SUCCESSFUL
PEOPLE MANAGEMENT:
How to get and keep
good employees

CANADIAN SMALL BUSINESS SERIES

SUCCESSFUL PEOPLE MANAGEMENT:
How to get and keep good employees

Ross E. Smith

A FINANCIAL POST / MACMILLAN BOOK

Many thanks to my wife, Helen, and my daughters, Carolyn and Cindy

Canadian Cataloguing in Publication Data

Smith, Ross E., date
 Successful people management
(Canadian small business series)
Includes index.
ISBN 0-7705-1648-3 pa.
1. Personnel management. I. Title. II. Series.
HF5549.S65   658.3   C78-001273-9

Printed and bound in Canada for
The Macmillan Company of Canada Limited
70 Bond Street, Toronto, Ontario M5B 1X3

CONTENTS

SUCCESSFUL
PEOPLE MANAGEMENT:
How to get and keep
good employees

INTRODUCTION

Every organization has a purpose. Whether you are in the profit-making or the public-service sector, you need human assets and physical assets in order to meet the organization's objectives. The aim of this book is to help you to manage your human assets more effectively. After all, human assets are a major cost, a potential source of increased productivity (or lack of it), and the cause of most of a manager's problems.

Regardless of your job function and the size of your organization or department, you can use the Model for Human Resource Management in managing your human resources.

Model for Human Resource Management

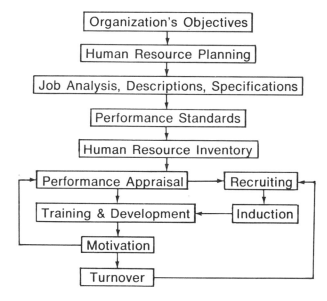

When using this model ask yourself these questions:

1. What is the importance of human resources in achieving the objectives of my department or organization?
2. What are the human requirements for each job function?
3. How can the effectiveness of human assets be measured?
4. What skills do my employees have?
5. How can I find out how well each employee is performing?
6. How can employees be developed to use their potential and skills?
7. Why do people work?
8. What are the rewards employees receive for working for me?
9. How can I get increased performance without increasing wages and salaries?
10. How can I reduce lateness, absenteeism, and turnover?
11. Where can I find and how do I select new employees?
12. How should I handle collective bargaining?

Use the Table of Contents and the Index for helping you to find answers to these and other questions for your specific needs. Make this book work for you: underline, write notes in the margins, fill out the worksheets, or make worksheets of your own.

ROSS E. SMITH

Successful People Management

1

PLANNING YOUR HUMAN RESOURCES

THE IMPORTANCE OF HUMAN RESOURCES

All organizations, whether profit-making or non-profit, are in business to supply a product or service. The success of the organization will depend on the abilities of all employees to meet their performance objectives.

The success of every manager and supervisor will depend on the ability to satisfy the needs of the organization, while also satisfying the needs of the personnel—the human resources. When these needs are compatible, the manager will achieve what every organization wants: employees motivated to achieve the organization's goals.

The human assets can make or break any organization. Therefore, the ultimate success of the organization will depend on skills in managing human resources: planning, evaluating, recruiting, training, rewarding, and directing. Another reason for the importance of human resources is that salaries and wages are the largest cash expenditure in most organizations, especially in service organizations.

Many managers and supervisors say that most of their problems are people problems. And many managers fail, not because of a lack of technical expertise, but because of an inability to effectively manage their subordinates.

Every organization has policies concerning its human resources. Often, these policies are oral, informal, and made up for each new situation or change in a situation. For more effective management, these policies should be related to the organization's objectives (short and long term) and put in writing. When objectives change, policies should also change.

Regardless of what your product or service is, you are also in the people business. Your survival and growth depend on your ability to recruit and use human resources effectively. Managers in small organizations have an advantage because they are directly involved in the short- and long-term activities of their employees. They can have a great influence on the successful managing of human assets and therefore on the success of the entire organization.

HOW TO PLAN YOUR HUMAN RESOURCES

Planning human-resource needs is tied in with the overall planning for your business. Are you planning to expand? to add new products or services? or to change the nature of your business? How many persons (at various levels, departments, and locations) will be needed to meet the objectives of your organization this year? How many will be needed next year?

Just as you use budgets for financial planning and forecasting, you should budget for people. Exhibit 1-1 is an example of a Human Resources Planning Worksheet which you can adapt to your own needs. If your organization is too big for one page, use separate pages for office, factory, or other large departments. In your people plan, list all the job categories or functions needed to operate your business (Column 1). Also list what new skills and functions are planned and which ones will be eliminated.

When completing Column 2, don't count the number of persons you have; after all, you might be over- or understaffed. Just show the number of people you need. (You can qualify the numbers by showing full-time F, part-time P, and temporary T, workers.)

Depending on the nature of your business, seasonal patterns, planned expansion, and so on, pick dates which will reflect changes in your work force (Columns 3, 4, 5, etc.). Your planning should also allow for employee turnover. Remember, turnover can be either voluntary or involuntary: some people leave when you least expect them to. You can't show turnover on your Planning Worksheet, but you have to keep it in mind when planning recruiting. Because of uncertainties, many managers fill out their worksheets in pencil and make contingency plans.

Exhibit 1-1
Human Resources Planning Worksheet

1 Job Classification	2 How many persons needed for present business volume? F　P　T	3 How many in 6 months? Date:	4 How many in 1 year? Date:	5 How many in 2 years? Date:
A. *Management:* 　General Manager 　Financial Manager 　Service Manager 　Factory Manager 　Supervisors				
B. *Office Skills:* 　Accountant 　Bookkeeper 　Receptionist 　Secretary 　Order Service				
C. *Factory Skills:* 　Machinists 　Maintenance 　Quality control 　Shipping 　Drivers				

Date Prepared _____

JOB ANALYSIS, JOB DESCRIPTIONS, JOB SPECIFICATIONS, AND PERFORMANCE STANDARDS

Having decided on the job categories, you should now prepare a job description for each category or job classification. You might need one or many employees in the same category. The same job description will apply to all of those employees in that category.

Some organizations function without formal or written job descriptions: employees do whatever the boss decides they should do. Also, some work situations are unpredictable or unstable. Whatever work has to be done is done by the nearest person or the one who is most qualified. Other organizations require more structure. Whether or not you write the job description, each employee must know:

1. What are the duties or responsibilities.
2. What authority the job carries.
3. What are the performance standards or objectives for the job.

The advantages of actually writing out the job descriptions are many. First, the manager of a small business needs to have the right person in the right job. Only large organizations can afford the luxury of making mistakes in selection and placement. Second, writing helps clarify thoughts. Third, a written description can be used as a common reference by all involved persons. And fourth, a written description can be used for performance appraisal.

Your objective should be to carefully and thoroughly analyze your needs—and you should use the same care and thoroughness in recruiting.

Let's agree on some terminology before you begin writing.

Job Description: This can also be referred to as a position description. It describes duties and responsibilities.

Job Specification: This shows the qualifications needed by the person who will be performing the duties outlined in the job description.

A job description, then, describes the job; a job specification descṛibes the person needed to perform the job. Some employers use the terms interchangeably; some combine both in the same written document. Do whatever works well for you, but, when using the terminology with other persons, be certain to explain what the terms mean to you.

Job Analysis

You have several choices in the way you can find out about a job already being performed. First, you can observe the person performing the job. Second, you can study the machines and equipment used and the physical environment where the job is performed. Third, you can interview the person who performs the job. And fourth, you can have that person complete a Job Analysis Questionnaire. (Exhibit 1-2 is a guide. Make changes to suit the needs of your organization.)

When you ask employees to describe their jobs, you can expect them to emphasize high-status items, minimize or leave out low-status and routine items, and describe qualifications they have rather than the qualifications needed to perform the job. Don't worry if the employees are not objective; they're being human. Therefore, the Job Analysis Questionnaire should be used in conjunction with one or more of the other methods mentioned. This self-analysis shows how employees see and feel about their jobs.

Job Description

Who should prepare the job description? You can, the department manager or supervisor can, or the employee already performing the job can. But whoever prepares the job description, be certain that it is factual and complete.

What should be included in a job description? Exhibit 1-3 is an outline which you should adapt to your needs. Exhibit 1-4 is an outline of a Job Specification. For some jobs you could simply show objectives or results to be expected, authority to be used to achieve the objectives, and resources to be used. You would still need a Job Specification. The person who was hired or assigned to the job could then (if necessary) write the job description.

Performance Standards

These standards can be designed to meet the requirements of the job and the abilities of the person doing the job. Job standards could be based on the performance to be expected from a fully qualified person. But a new employee or one who lacks the necessary skills and experience may not be able to perform

Exhibit 1-2
Job Analysis Questionnaire

You know the job well because you are the person who does the job. The information you provide will be used in preparing a Job Description for your job.

Guidelines:
1. Write in your own words. Don't be concerned about grammar and spelling. It's the information that's important.
2. Be brief and concise. You don't have to use complete sentences.
3. Be accurate. Just show the facts. Don't write what you think the job should be. Just describe the job as it is.

Job Title of Position _____

Prepared by _____ Date _____

1. What are your duties and responsibilities? Make a list. Put the most important duties first. Estimate the percentage of time spent on the major duties.

_____

_____

_____

2. What are the skills and knowledge needed to perform your job?

_____

_____

_____

List the skills separately:
a. Manual skills _____
b. Physical skills _____
c. Mental skills _____
d. Supervisory skills _____
e. Management skills _____

3. How does your job fit in with other jobs? How are the jobs related?

_____

_____

_____

4. With whom do you have to communicate and why? Suggestions: fellow employees, work team (co-operative job), subordinates, other departments, customers, suppliers, the public.

_____

_____

_____

cont'd

_____

5. List anything else about your job that you think is important.

_____

_____

_____

Exhibit 1-3
Job Description

Prepared by: _____   Date: _____
Approved by: _____   Date: _____
Reviewed by: _____   Date: _____

Job Title: _____
Purpose of job (objective) _____

_____

Duties (list the responsibilities in the order of importance or percentage of time spent):
1. _____
2. _____
3. _____
4. _____
5. _____
Authority: _____
Equipment operated: _____
Working conditions: _____
Working hours: _____
Supervisory Duties: ⎫
                    ⎬ draw an organization chart
Supervised by: ⎭
Relationships to other jobs (contacts within the organization and outside): _____
Standards of Performance (Quality, quantity, cost, time): _____

_____

Training:
What has to be learned during probation?

_____

What has to be learned to upgrade the employee?

_____

Career Opportunities: _____

```
Exhibit 1-4
Job Specification*

    Prepared by: _____        Date: _____
    Approved by: _____        Date: _____
    Reviewed by: _____        Date: _____

Job Title: _____
Qualifications: _____
    1.  Education: _____
    2.  Training: _____
    3.  Experience: _____
    4.  Physical skills: _____
    5.  Mental skills: _____
    6.  Special skills (languages, creativity): _____
    7.  Professional designation or licence: _____
    8.  Interpersonal skills (personality): _____
    9.  Oral communications: _____
   10.  Written communications: _____
   11.  Personal grooming: _____
   12.  Supervisory (leadership): _____
   13.  Managerial (planning, organizing, decision making): ____
   14.  Potential (upgrading, promotion): _____

* Job Specifications must not violate the Human Rights Code.
```

up to standard; this person should be trained to meet the expected standards.

Some persons will be able to exceed the standards. Should the standards be changed to match this superior performance? Probably not, especially if the standards were objectively established. Note that the emphasis is on performance or what the person will be expected to do. These standards do not refer to materials, equipment, or product specifications.

Engineered standards These standards are objectively set through time-and-motion studies and other forms of work measurement. These standards can be based on estimated equipment performance and what a well-trained machine operator should be able to produce.

Non-engineered standards These standards are more subjectively set because they are based on management experience and feelings as well as supervisor-subordinate agreement.

These standards also apply to jobs that have a variety of duties, some of which cannot be specifically measured. Service jobs are in this category. Standards are also based on what an incumbent or predecessor has done.

Whenever possible, performance standards should be based on one or more of *quantity, quality, cost,* and *time.* Standards should always describe the results expected. Both the supervisor and the employee then know how the employee's performance will be evaluated.

These standards are also useful in recruiting: whoever is doing the interviewing can refer to the job description and the standards of performance. The applicant can be told specifically what the duties, responsibilities, and working conditions are as well as the facts on how the employee's performance will be evaluated. Unless the information is confidential, the job description could be shown to the applicant. Many applicants just looking for any job will screen themselves out when confronted with the realities of the work situation; trained or skilled employees planning to leave their jobs and work for you should be clearly shown that you are a results-oriented organization.

Your own employees who would like to transfer or be promoted should be shown the job description of the job for which they are applying. Both you and the employee can then be more objective in deciding on the transfer or promotion. Both of you can discuss the standards of performance rather than the employee's personality, loyalty, and other characteristics not directly related to performance. The standards should be the normal result that can be attained by a trained or experienced person.

In addition to being realistic and attainable, the standard should also be challenging: the employee should be able to do the job if willing to work at it. Performance standards should start at the top of the organization, then be developed for every job down through the hierarchy.

Exhibit 1-5 is a worksheet for writing performance standards. It should be used by you in setting standards for your job. Your managers and supervisors should do the same for their jobs. You and your management team must set standards for yourselves before you try to set standards for others.

Terminology: You can use Standards of Performance or Performance Objective(s). A Job Description could include performance Standards. This combination is sometimes termed a *Job Performance Guide.* The latter is then a description of the whole job and the expected results.

Regardless of terminology, both the supervisor and the employee should know what is expected of the employee.

HUMAN-RESOURCES INVENTORY

After you have completed your Human Resources Planning Worksheet, Job Descriptions, and Job Specifications, your next step is to answer this question: What are the skills and potentials of my employees? The objective is to compare what you have with what you need. In order to know what you have, you must take inventory; in order to take inventory, you must count and categorize what you have. But before you categorize, you must decide what you want to know about your employees.

The following list suggests items which you can modify, delete, or add to in devising your human-resource inventory. Make your list specific to your organization's needs. (Do not violate the Human Rights Code when compiling your list.)

Job classification
Education
Training
Experience
Special skills, i.e. languages
Professional designations or licences
Equipment skills
Physical skills, i.e. health

Mental skills
Communication skills:
  oral
  written
  interpersonal
Supervisory skills
Management skills, i.e. planning, organizing
Hobbies and special interests
Off-the-job activities (exclude religious and ethnic activities)
Potential, i.e. trainability
Career plan

After deciding what you want, how are you going to get the information?

Much of the information is probably in your personal records: resumés, application forms, performance appraisals. Some of the information is in your head and in the heads of your managers and supervisors. You might know a little about everyone and a lot about a few persons. Another source is the employee; explain to employees that many people have skills, experiences, potential, and ambitions the organization doesn't know anything about. Employees should be assured that the objective of the inventory is to help both the employees and the organization—not to increase the employees' workload. Management's knowledge of this information could result in employees being upgraded, given more responsibility and authority, transferred, or promoted.

The organization's growth and expansion will depend on the availability of qualified persons. When there are vacancies, employees should always be considered first before recruiting outside the organization.

Exhibit 1-6 is an example of a form for obtaining data from employees. A long list of possible skills and experiences will show employees what you are specifically looking for. Such a form is easy for employees to complete.

However, a disadvantage of such a list is that some employees might have very little information to put on the inventory. These employees might feel inferior because they have little to contribute. Some will use their imaginations to exaggerate their qualifications or invent fictitious data. An alternative is to make a general statement of what you are looking for and let the employee volunteer the necessary information. The disadvantage is that your request omits a specific list.

A solution is to compile a detailed list—but don't show it to the employee. The supervisor can interview each employee and

Exhibit 1-6
Human-Resources Inventory

Employee's Name: _____ Date: _____
Information compiled by: _____

Purpose: To identify the skills, experiences, potential, and career plans of each employee.

Use of information: This information can benefit both the employee and the organization by identifying employees who want and are capable of being upgraded, trained, or promoted.

Categories: This list is specifically detailed so that all pertinent information can be identified. No one person is expected to have all or even most of these categories.

Do not supply information of a religious or ethnic nature. However, an employee could volunteer information that he/she is an officer in a religious organization without revealing the religious denomination.

1. Education _____
2. Training _____
3. Experience _____
4. Special skills _____
5. Professional designation or licence _____
6. Supervisory or leadership skills _____
7. Management skills: planning, organizing _____
8. Communication skills:
   oral _____
   written _____
9. Is there anything else you would like the organization to know about you? _____
   _____

This inventory was planned to comply with the Human Rights Code. Do not supply information that you think violates your rights to privacy.

use the list as a guide in asking questions. To avoid suspicion and defensiveness, let the employee see the inventory sheet that the supervisor is completing. You receive added benefits in interviewing each employee: the manager or supervisor gets to know more about each employee; also, employees know that management is treating them as individuals who are important to the organization.

Your Human Resource Inventory should be kept up to date. Encourage employees to tell their supervisor of any changes in the information that has been recorded. A supervisor with a good day-to-day relationship with employees will be able to gather pertinent new information.

A small organization therefore has an advantage over a large organization. The Human Resource Inventory can be a perpetual rather than an annual checkup. This up-to-date inventory can reduce costs of recruiting and training by finding out all the skills your employees have. They may already have acquired skills on or off the job you don't know about, so you might have the person you want already in your organization.

Does every organization need a Human Resources Inventory system?

1. An organization of 50 to 75 employees will probably need an inventory system.
2. A system will be needed for small organizations if the jobs are complex or varied.
3. Geographic dispersion necessitates an inventory because of less management-employee personal contact.
4. An organization in a market and/or business which frequently changes has to keep an up-to-date inventory.
5. An inventory will be needed by a growing organization that needs more employees.

Your Human-Resource Inventory should be compared with the Human-Resources Planning Worksheet. Compare the employees you have with the Job Classifications: are you understaffed, over-staffed, or just right? What are your expectations on voluntary and involuntary turnover: how many employees will quit, be fired, become sick, or retire? What skills and qualifications do your employees have that are not being used? What training and experience will employees need for upgrading and promotion? Should the organization be restructured to make better use of the available talent? (Example: combining two jobs or departments to make use of the varied skills of an employee or manager.)

A small organization should be able to show projections. (See Exhibit 1-7 for an example.) Make this form specific to your needs. Don't worry about making projections that six months from now could prove you wrong. Do your planning on the best available information as well as on your own experience and the experience of others. (A manager's job is to make decisions: if judgement wasn't needed, an organization wouldn't need managers.) But be prepared for surprises. You know why you made your plan, so your experience will indicate how accurate your predictions will be.

Exhibit 1-7
Projection of Human-Resources Needs

Date: _____

Job Classification	1 Number needed now	2 Number we have	3 Excess or shortage Use +, −, 0	4 Estimated turnover in next 6 months	Total of 3 & 4	Action to be taken: H = Hire (show date) W = Wait (show reason)
Office Manager	1	1	0	0	0	
Accounting Manager	1	0	−1	0	−1	H (date)
Service Manager	1	0	−1	0	−1	H (date)
Bookkeeper	1	1	0	0	0	
Typist	5	4	−1	−1	−2	W (until vacancy occurs)
Driver	2	2	0	−1	−1	W (until vacancy occurs)
Equipment Operator etc.	10	12	+2	−3	−1	W (until no longer overstaffed then recruit 1 even if it means we will again be overstaffed)

Compiled by: _____ Date: _____

Reviewed by: _____ Date: _____

THE CASH VALUE OF HUMAN RESOURCES

Today is a beautiful day. Not only is the weather good, but I also feel good. And business has been good—I'm going to have a great year.

That's a good reason for sleeping in and arriving a little late. And why not? I'm the boss. Besides, I have a responsible work team. They don't need me to unlock the door, turn on the lights, and begin another productive day.

That's odd. The lights aren't on. Maybe there's a power outage. Or my watch is wrong and I'm an hour early.

No. I'm not late. But the place is dark inside. What's this? The door's locked. This is crazy.

Notes are fastened to the front door. They read like this:

Dear boss:

Everyday one of us is usually away for one reason or another. Today is the day I thought I'd take off.

Please don't take it personally. I like you and the organization. But I decided that maybe you could get along without me today.

Just think of today as Saturday or Sunday. I'll see you tomorrow. Or the next day.

(signed) The Employee

After a quick check of the signatures on the notes, I realized something horrible—everyone's away today!

Just then the light did come on.

"Wake up. It's time to get to work."

Oh what a dream! What a bad dream!

"What's the matter, dear? You don't look so good. Maybe you should stay home today."

Stay home! "What if everyone stayed home today?"

"Are you crazy? That will never happen. Go have your breakfast."

"No. I've got to get to work right away. I've got a strange feeling."

Suppose it wasn't a dream. Suppose no one came to work today. What would happen to your business? Worse still, suppose every one of your employees handed in their notice today. How long would it take to:

1. Recruit new people to fill all the jobs?
2. Train the new employees?
3. Integrate the new people into a competent work team?
4. Achieve satisfactory productivity?

What would all this cost?

A survey of top management in several organizations indicated that the cost would be anywhere from two to ten times the cost of the annual payroll. Most of the managers surveyed said the cost would be three to five times their annual payroll.

What would be the cost to your organization?

My annual payroll is $_____

Cost of rebuilding human assets: payroll × 3

Total: $_____

That's a lot of money! Let's use some round figures to further illustrate this point:

Annual payroll	$100,000
Cost of rebuilding	× 3
	$300,000

If your payroll is estimated at, say, about five times profit, then profits are $20,000. Therefore, your human assets are worth about fifteen times your profit. So your human resources are important —and expensive to replace.

Human-Resources Accounting

Putting your human assets on the balance sheet is a way of quantifying an intangible asset. In the above example, under assets you would show: Employees $300,000. You might also want to make provisions for depreciation, appreciation, and re-placement.

Productivity and Profit

Let's use the same figures as above (Payroll $100,000; Profit $20,000), but let's be more conservative on replacement cost ($200,000 instead of $300,000). Suppose your employees improve their human productivity by 1% with no increase in costs. This 1% is worth $2000. And this $2000 is a 10% increase in your profit. A 5% increase in productivity would be worth $10,000— a 50% increase in your profits.

Depending on the nature of your business, there could be two hidden costs:

1. The underuse of machines, equipment, and other physical assets.
2. The underuse of human assets.

For most organizations the underuse of human assets is more expensive than the underuse of other assets.

Many managers make statements like, "People are our greatest asset." These same managers (and accountants) know the dollar value of their physical plant and equipment, costs of acquisition, repairs, maintenance, depreciation, and scrap value or replacement. Any changes are noted in the account books. These changes have a direct effect on profits and losses. "Our greatest asset" should also be quantified. This quantification, imperfect though it may be, might impress more managers about the dollar value of their human assets. Any changes in this value will directly affect costs and profits.

It is traditional to calculate return on investment (ROI) from capital investments. But ROI should also be calculated for human assets, especially for service organizations. Another way to look at valuation is to answer these questions: What would your organization be worth if it was to be sold as a going concern? What would it be worth if it was sold without the employees?

The selling price would probably not be based only on the value of the tangible assets. The seller and buyer would also calculate the capitalization of the human assets. After all, anyone with money can buy a building, machines, and equipment, but what would it cost to staff the organization? That's the real cost that will help to determine the selling price.

COSTS OF HUMAN RESOURCES

Historical costs are a method of valuing your investment in human assets. These assets are measured at the time of their acquisition or occurrence. Although this value can be outdated, it is consistent with other accounting methods. This system is also simple, cheap, and practical.

1. **Recruiting costs:**
   Advertising
   Employment-agency fees
   Time for:
     screening
     interviewing

testing
health examination
reference checking
Incidental expenses
The costs of unsuccessful applicants must be added to the costs of recruiting the successful job applicants.

2. **Induction costs:**
Orientation
Informal training: adapting the specific skills of the new employee to the job requirements.
Time for the new employee to reach the standards of performance.
Effect of the new employee on the productivity of other employees especially in co-operative work groups.

3. **Training and development costs:**
Formal education and training courses.
Seminars
Upgrading
Reassignment
Promotion

4. **Lost opportunity costs:**
Absenteeism
Accidents
Illness
Turnover
Loss of productivity

Some of these costs are easier to measure than others, but all of these costs have an effect on the value of your human assets.

When calculating return on investment, a labor-intensive organization should consider the proportion of human assets to non-human assets. Also, historical costs may distort the current value of your human resources. Employees who increase their productivity should be shown as appreciating in value. Inflation, remember, will also affect the replacement value of all employees.

After incurring costs of recruiting, induction, training, and development, an employee may terminate employment before that employee's productivity has made this investment worthwhile. This turnover often happens when long training periods are involved. Apprentices are an example of this turnover.

Replacement Cost

Exhibit 1-8 is a form that could be used in calculating the cost of replacing an employee. Modify the form to suit your circumstances. When the form is well designed it will be easy for you or your designate to complete; the difficult part will be estimating the time and financial costs.

As a learning experience, all managers and supervisors should complete a Replacement Cost form at least once. These persons would then have a better understanding and appreciation of turnover costs and the effects of these costs on the valuation of human assets.

To the statement, "People are our most important asset," could be added, "People are our most costly asset."

Exhibit 1-8

Replacement Cost Worksheet

Department _____ Job Title _____ Date _____
Ex-Employee's Name _____
New Employee's Name _____
Instructions: 1. This form will be completed by the Department Manager.
            2. Some costs and savings will be accurate and others will be estimates. Try to be as accurate as possible.

	Time	Cost
A. Cost of ex-employee's departure:		
1. Severance pay (for time not worked):	_____	_____
2. Loss of output (while position vacant):	_____	_____
3. Disruption in dept. (productivity):	_____	_____
B. Cost of recruitment:		
1. Writing job specifications:	_____	_____
2. Internal search (promote or transfer another employee):	_____	_____
3. Contacting employment agency:	_____	_____
4. Employment agency fee:	_____	_____
5. Advertising:	_____	_____
6. Interviewing (Dept. Mgr.):	_____	_____
7. Department administration:	_____	_____

cont'd

C. Cost of induction:
   1. Department administration: _____   _____
   2. Training: _____   _____
   3. Loss of output (during training):
      (Do not duplicate item A2).   _____   _____
   4. Productivity (until competent):   _____   _____
                                                 Total Cost $ _____

Time: 1. From time of vacancy
         until new employee's arrival _____ (weeks, months)
     2. From time employee arrives until
         productivity is satisfactory   _____ (weeks, months)
               Total time (1 + 2)   _____ (weeks, months)

D. Other costs:
   1. Morale of other employees.
   2. Department productivity (ex-employee may have been in a work group).

E. Savings:
   1. Morale may go up if ex-employee unpopular.
   2. Productivity may go up if ex-employee incompetent, especially if a member of a work group.
   3. Pay of ex-employee (while position vacant) $_____
   4. Fringe benefits:
      a. Holiday pay (Ex-employee may have been entitled to 3 weeks, while new employee only gets 2 weeks.)
        $_____
      b. Pension fund $_____
      c. Profit sharing, bonuses $_____
      d. Insurance $_____
      e. Other $_____
      Total savings (tangibles) $_____
   Net cost of turnover (tangibles) $_____

2
RECRUITING: STRATEGY

Performance Appraisal

A performance appraisal, the evaluation of an employee's performance, is important because management wants to know how well each employee is performing, while employees want to know how well they're doing and what management thinks of their performances. A performance appraisal can be used by management in making decisions concerning a pay increase, upgrading, transfer, promotion, training and development, demotion, termination.

Performance appraisals can be either formal or informal. The informal appraisal involves the day-to-day contact between manager/supervisor and employee. A working relationship is established so that the manager rewards and punishes the employee on the day-to-day activities. Formal appraisals are carried out periodically (three months, six months, or a year); a written report is made of each employee's personal record on the job.

If a manager has a good day-to-day relationship with each employee, the employees will know how they're doing and what the manager thinks of their performances. The formal (periodic) appraisal, therefore, will not include any information the employee doesn't already know. As a result, the formal appraisal is a confirmation of what the manager and employee both know. If the information in the written report comes as a surprise to the employee, something is wrong with the day-to-day communication between the two.

Why should a formal appraisal be written? Because writing requires thought and planning, because words are carefully chosen for understanding and impact, and because the appraisal is a record which can be used for common reference.

Who should be responsible for preparing the written appraisal?

Both the manager and the employee should be responsible. Both should individually prepare a written report. The reports should then be compared.

What happens if the two agree? Agreement obviously indicates no differences in opinion; the appraisal is therefore acceptable to both. (A cynic could say that although both agreed, both could be wrong. In fact, many employees rate themselves lower than managers do.)

What happens if the manager and the employee disagree? That is, the manager rates the employee lower than the employee does. If the disagreement is minor, the differences can usually be resolved to the satisfaction of both; often the wording or the terminology can be changed. When two persons rate one of them on something as subjective as performance, minor disagreements are to be expected.

However, if the disagreement is major, something is wrong with the manager's or the employee's perception of the employee's performance. Again, serious disagreement shouldn't happen if their day-to-day communications are effective.

If the disagreement can't be resolved, the manager can always make an arbitrary decision. As an example, three umpires were asked how they called balls and strikes at a baseball game. The rookie umpire said, "I call them as I see them." The veteran umpire said, "I call them as they are." The senior umpire said, "They are what I call them." You shouldn't become an umpire (or a manager) if you want to win a popularity contest. You have to do what is right—or what you think is right.

What factors should be included in the appraisal? The key word is performance: how well did the employee perform the job? Compare the employee's performance with the standards of performance or performance objectives that were established for the job. The appraisal is easy if the performance is quantifiable in terms of quantity, quality, cost, or time—and if the records are accurate.

The appraisal should give reasons for the results. The reasons, good or bad, could be attributed to circumstances and events over which the employee had control as well as the ones over which the employee had no control (or a combination of both). Give credit or blame fairly. Performance which is not quantifiable will have to be described and will be more subjective: "I call them as I see them."

Other items which traditionally appear on appraisal reports are co-operativeness, initiative, dependability, reliability, job knowledge, personal qualities, ability to work with others, appearance, attitude, and willingness. How can these qualities be measured? Not easily, if at all. Unreliability can be measured by lateness, absenteeism, and illness. Appearance can be described, especially if the employee wears a uniform.

But which of these qualitative items are necessary for effective job performance? Promptness and appearance may be important for a service advisor. Some of these qualitative characteristics may be desirable in all employees, but only evaluate them if they are important for job performance.

When conducting your appraisal interview, you will probably find that the employee agrees more readily with the quantitative than with the qualitative items.

Appraisal-Planning Worksheet

Use Exhibit 2-1 as a guide for your organization. First, make a list of all job classifications. Second, make a list of all performance standards for all jobs. Third, check off those standards which should be evaluated for each job. (The check marks will probably indicate that not all of the performance standards apply to all jobs.) The ideal solution would be to design an appraisal form for each job classification; the easy solution is to design one form to be used for appraising all jobs.

Performance-Appraisal Form

A suggested format is shown in Exhibit 2-2. The contents of this form would be prepared by the manager or supervisor. When the contents are prepared by the employee (self-evaluation), the employee would complete everything except the signature. The comments should include any specific circumstances concerning the employee's performance. Particular reference should be made to events that were or were not within the employee's control. The overall rating should be finalized as satisfactory or unsatisfactory. Some of the common errors in appraisal are listed in Exhibit 2-3.

Recommendations If the rating is satisfactory:
1. Has the employee reached the limit of ability?
2. Should the employee have more training or experience?
3. Should the employee be upgraded or promoted?

Exhibit 2-1

Appraisal Planning Worksheet
Performance Standards

Job Classification	Quantity	Quality	Cost	Time	Reliability	Job Knowledge	Personal Qualities	Interpersonal Skills	Oral Communications	Written Communications	Appearance	Attitude	Willingness	Co-operation	Initiative
General Manager															
Sales Manager															
Accountant															
Secretary															
Driver															
Machinist															
Etc.															

If the rating is unsatisfactory:
1. Should the employee have more training?
2. Should the employee be transferred?
3. Should the employee be terminated?

Appraisal Interview

What should you do to prepare for the interview? First, collect all the information you'll need at the interview: performance record, attendance record, and so on. Second, complete the rating form and make your evaluation; be honest and fair, because what you record could help or hurt someone. Third, based on your evaluation, decide whether the employee's overall performance is satisfactory or unsatisfactory.

If unsatisfactory, ask yourself if the performance could be improved. If the answer is yes, then plan ways for improvement.

Exhibit 2-2
Performance Appraisal

Name: _____

Job Classification: _____

Prepared by: _____ Date: _____

Period: (3 months, 6 months, 1 year)

Objective:
    To evaluate the employee's performance in relation to the Performance Objectives for this job classification.

Performance Objectives   *Employee's Performance*

1. Quantity:
2. Quality:
3. Cost:
4. Time:
5. Comments: _____

    _____

6. Rating: Satisfactory _____ or Unsatisfactory _____
7. Recommendations: _____

    _____

8. Signature: _____ Employee's Signature: _____

_____   _____

Manager or Supervisor
                ☐ I have read the appraisal.
                ☐ I understand the appraisal.
                ☐ I agree/disagree with the rating.
9. Employee's comments (use other side if necessary): _____

    _____

Exhibit 2-3

Errors in Appraisal and How to Overcome Them

We are human: what we see and hear is filtered through our experiences, outlook, and feelings. As a result, all appraisal is subjective. And all subjective appraisals will have errors. Here are some of the more common errors:

The halo effect Basing an overall appraisal on only one aspect of performance. Each standard of performance should be judged independently. But, if you don't like someone's personality, you might give a lower rating to the person's job performance. It's difficult to say, "I don't like her, but I like her work." Also, mistakes by good-looking and/or co-operative people are sometimes overlooked.

Here's what you can do to avoid being taken in by the halo effect:

1. Know the characteristics of each performance standard.
2. Rate each standard separately.
3. Keep in mind that your evaluation must be accurate because it will affect the employee and the organization.

Leniency No one wants to give someone else a low rating. It's easier to tell an employee the rating is good rather than bad. Your boss might also want an explanation if your subordinate has a low rating. Low ratings can lead to grievances, especially if employees are unionized.

Suggestions to prevent leniency:

1. Keep performance records.
2. Compare the employees performance with the performance objectives for the job.
3. Let the employee know immediately when performance is unsatisfactory—don't wait for the formal appraisal.
4. An inaccurate rating does not help you, the employee, or the organization.

Central tendency Rating an employee as "average," if he is a borderline case. An employee might think that he is better than average, but won't complain if he thinks he is below average. If the evaluator doesn't know how to evaluate the employee's performance, she feels safe in showing a rating of average.

If you can't rate an employee accurately:

1. Check the performance objectives. Are they clear and specific?
2. Keep better records.
3. Consider only two ratings: satisfactory or unsatisfactory— no one is average.

cont'd

> **Recent events**   It is human to remember what happened to-day and to forget what happened six months or a year ago. To help your memory, you should:
> 1. Keep records.
> 2. Refer to the records. Don't rely only on your memory.
> 3. Has the performance changed since the previous appraisal?
>
> **Outstanding events**   It is also human to remember something outstanding, either good or bad. The memory of that memorable event remains uppermost in our minds. To be fair, you should:
> 1. Refer to the records. Was the outstanding event an isolated incident or did it happen regularly?
> 2. Decide to what extent the employee caused the event. Was the outstanding event caused by good or bad luck?
> 3. Consider the likelihood of the event being repeated.

If the answer is no, then decide to accept low productivity, transfer the employee, or terminate the employee.

Fourth, decide on the objective of the interview. It could be to tell the employee how his or her performance compares with what was expected, to plan for improved performance, to set new objectives, or to transfer or terminate the employee. Whatever you decide, the employee must know how he or she is doing as well as what he or she must do and how to do it.

Fifth, plan what you're going to do and say. Here's a suggested sequence of events. Review the employee's strengths; review the employee's weaknesses; compare your evaluation with the employee's self-evaluation; think of training or improvement programs or whether to terminate the employee; and be ready to discuss new standards of performance.

The sixth and final preparation for the appraisal interview is to select a time and place for privacy, when and where the two of you can talk without interruption.

When conducting the interview, first tell the employee the purpose of the interview. Next, tell the employee what your evaluation of the employee's performance is: start with the good news, the employee's strengths, then break the bad news, the employee's weaknesses. Ask for and listen to the employee's comments about your appraisal and the employee's self-appraisal.

Try to come to an understanding of what both of you are saying. Clarify words and terminology. Don't assume the employee understands everything—but don't ask, "Do you understand?" because you're really asking the employee to admit to ignorance and/or stupidity. Instead, ask, "Is there anything I haven't made clear?" or "Is there anything I've left out?" Make sure you both eventually reach agreement on what's been said (and sign the rating form).

Finally, plan objectives and development or training—termination, if necessary. If your appraisal is adverse, you could tell the employee, "If your performance (or behaviour) becomes satisfactory in thirty days, I'll destroy this adverse appraisal. It won't be put on your record. A new appraisal showing your improvement and satisfactory performance will be put on your record instead."

Summary Appraisal interviews don't have to be emotionally upsetting to the supervisor or the employee, if you:

1. Establish performance standards which are clearly understood and attainable.
2. Maintain an effective day-to-day relationship with the employee.
3. Base your appraisal on specific facts about performance.

Appraise what the employee has done, not the employee's personality.

The appraisal interview is completed and you're probably glad it is. But you have one or two more things to do. First, you might want to confirm in writing what you and the employee have agreed on. Second, you should rate yourself on how well you think you conducted the interview. Exhibit 2-4 is a checklist you can use for this purpose.

RECRUITING STRATEGY

Your recruiting methods will depend on:

1. Whether you have a choice. You might have to use a union hiring hall, for instance.
2. How much time and effort you want to spend. To save time, an employment agency can function as your personnel manager.
3. How much money you're willing to spend. For instance, do you want to pay the employment agency's fee?
4. How qualified you are to assess applicants. You may know manufacturing, for instance, but maybe not how to evaluate people.
5. Whether you want everyone (employees, friends, relatives, competitors, unemployed persons, and so on) to know you

Exhibit 2-4

Manager's or Supervisor's Appraisal of
Her or His Own Interview Performance

	Yes	No
Before the interview:		
1. I had all the necessary information.	___	___
2. I completed the Performance-Appraisal Form.	___	___
3. I planned what I was going to say.	___	___
4. I picked a private place for the interview.	___	___
5. I think I was well prepared.	___	___
During the interview:		
6. At the start I put the employee at ease.	___	___
7. I explained the purpose of the interview.	___	___
8. I reviewed his/her strengths.	___	___
9. I reviewed his/her weaknesses.	___	___
10. I listened to his/her comments about:		
a. My appraisal of him/her	___	___
b. His/Her self-appraisal	___	___
11. I understood what we both were saying.	___	___
12. I got agreement of what we both were saying.	___	___
13. I/We established future performance objectives.	___	___
After the interview:		
14. I accomplished my objective.	___	___
15. I am satisfied with the way I conducted the interview.	___	___
16. Using hindsight, these are the things I should have done differently:		

need employees. If you put an ad in the paper, you might receive 70 applications.

If you select the wrong person, you could have a number of problems that will affect your organization for months—or years, if the person isn't replaced. The wrong person will not meet the standards of performance for the job. The wrong person could adversely affect the performance of other employees. The wrong person will cause most of your supervising problems. There are people who have the qualifications (skills, knowledge, and personality) that your organization needs. You *can* recruit the right people, but you must be prepared and willing to make the time and effort needed to do the job properly.

Recruitment offers management an opportunity to improve an organization, especially if you use a rational approach. Here are guidelines for using a rational approach to recruitment:

1. Know what you are looking for. Refer to the job description and job specifications. Concentrate on the essential qualifications needed. Ignore all non-essential qualifications.
2. Consider only a few applicants. If your advertisement attracts many persons, it is an indication that
   a. the qualifications for the job are too low, or
   b. the rewards are too high (or local unemployment is high). Conversely, if your advertisement attracts no one, it could mean that:
   a. the qualifications for the job are too high, or
   b. the rewards are too low.

If there are many applicants, you might try to find the best possible one among them by comparing one person with another. By picking the best out of many, you will probably get someone who is overqualified. You may be happy because you have found the best, but how will the best feel as an underemployed employee? Unless you are planning to give this employee more and more responsibility, be prepared for the day when this employee quits—it will happen fairly soon.

Applicants should not be compared with each other. Each applicant should be compared to the job specifications. Your decision should be that the person is either suitable for the job or unsuitable for the job. This decision should be made on each person before you consider the next one. If you have only one suitable person, then you should offer the job to that person. If you have two or three suitable candidates, rank them in the order of suitability. Offer the job to Person 1. If Person 1 declines, offer the job to Person 2, and so on. If everyone declines, you have a problem: you will have to go through the whole recruitment process again. Before making your job offer, make certain that the candidate clearly understands the job description and the standards of performance. The candidate should be told truthfully about the duties, responsibilities, objectives, opportunities, status, and so on—and in this situation, it is better to undersell than to oversell.

SELECTION BY MOTIVATION

Which assumption is correct?
1. Ability causes performance, or
2. Motivation causes performance.

Ability is defined as what a person can do. *Motivation* is defined as what a person will do. Performance is really the combination of ability and motivation as well as the characteristics of the job situation.

Most personnel-selection techniques are designed to determine an applicant's ability to do the job. After the person is hired, management then uses techniques of motivation (financial and non-financial rewards) to ensure that the person will meet the performance objectives of the job. But new employees have established their motivational characteristics as well as their abilities before they are hired.

Motivating a person would be much easier if you could determine *before hiring* what motivates a person. No magic formula, test, or machine will determine motivation, but you have to try to select for motivation. If not, you will have to rely almost completely on motivation-arousal techniques after the person is hired.

What should you do? You have to determine:
1. What behavioural patterns are necessary for successful job performance?
2. Which applicants have the needs or motives that will produce the required performance?

You can't see needs or motives. But they can be deduced from a person's behaviour.

Let's suppose that applicants have revealed the following variety of behaviours or activities:
1. Participate in relaxed small talk.
2. Take calculated risks.
3. Try to influence others.
4. Set challenging goals for themselves.
5. Want feedback on their performances.
6. Status is important for them.
7. Try hard to be liked.
8. Want to dominate others.
9. Try hard to reach goals.
10. Prefer positions of influence.
11. Try to get along well with others.
12. Try to control the means of influence.

How would you classify these 12 items under the:
Need for achievement: _____
Need for affiliation: _____
Need for power: _____

Decide which of the 12 items should go opposite each of the 3 needs. Compare your answers with the ones in the middle of page 34.

No one person will have a predominance of all of these characteristics, but some will have more than one. It is most likely that a person will only have the required job behaviour if that person has a tendency to perform in the expected manner.

The place to begin is by analyzing the job to be performed:

1. To what extent does successful job performance depend on the employee:
   a. Setting personal goals?
   b. Accepting responsibility for results?
   c. Taking calculated risks?
   d. Wanting frequent feedback on performance?
   e. Getting recognition for achievement?
   f. Adjusting personal goals?

2. To what extent does successful job performance depend on:
   a. Co-operation among employees?
   b. Frequent interpersonal contacts?
   c. Ability to get along well with others?

3. To what extent does successful job performance depend on the employee:
   a. Trying to influence others?
   b. Trying to dominate others?
   c. Compelling others to do what he wants?
   d. Dominating others?
   e. Wanting status and a position of influence?

Most jobs require a mixture of behaviours related to achievement, affiliation, and power. However, successful performance will probably depend on emphasizing one set of behaviours.

Tests can measure a person's need for achievement, affiliation, and power. These tests may not be suitable or practical for use in small businesses, however. The assessment of applicants must then be based on questions and answers at the job interview, checking with former employers, and, for recent graduates, checking with teachers or instructors.

Research has been conducted on small organizations to determine how the needs of the chief executive affected the organization's performance. Research discovered several types of corporate personalities. Some organizations had increased production, sales and profits. They were continuing to expand and enter new markets. The chief executive evaluated employees on their job performance. The competent were rewarded with money and opportunities for advancement. The incompetent were terminated. Success was based on achievement. Other organizations were not growing or growing slowly. Management picked subordinates who could be dominated. Responsibility was not shared. Employees were blamed for failure, but never praised or credited with success. Security was more important than taking risks. Success was based on power.

According to the study, chief executives of the highest-performing organizations were persons with a high need for achievement and a moderate need for power, while chief executives of the moderately successful organizations were persons with a high need for affiliation and a moderate need for achievement. Also, chief executives of the more stagnant organizations were persons with a high need for achievement and a high need for power. Organizations that depend on a high need for power usually produce autocratic or authoritarian behaviour in their leaders. This need for power could minimize or stifle the need for achievement.

Such research is not conclusive because individuals and organizations are too complicated for accurate analysis. But for those who want a simple answer to a complex problem, here is what the research indicates: the most successful person (especially in management and marketing) is high in achievement motivation, low in power motivation, and high in the need for affiliation.

On-the-Job Performance

You can verify your success in assessing applicants by observing their job performance. Needs and motives are invisible. But you can observe behaviour:
1. What does the employee want?
2. What does the employee do?
3. What does the employee talk about: the job? people? power?
4. Does the employee set challenging goals?
5. Does the employee accept responsibility for results?
6. What does the employee do with feedback?
7. What risks does the employee take?
8. Does the employee prefer small talk?

9. Does the employee try hard to be liked?
10. Does the employee prefer frequent interpersonal contacts?
11. Does the employee try to influence and dominate others?
12. Does the employee put great emphasis on winning?
13. Does the employee want status?

Coffeebreak and lunchtime discussions can tell you how people feel about their jobs, their problems, and what characteristics are needed for success.

The more you learn about your employees, the more successful you will be as a manager—but don't try to be an amateur psychologist: accept people for who and what they are. Don't try to analyze why people do what they do; even the experts aren't certain. Some of these "experts" could be your employees. And guess who they're analyzing?

Answers to questionnaire:
Need for achievement: 2, 4, 5, 9
Need for affiliation: 1, 7, 11
Need for power: 3, 6, 8, 10, 12

SOURCES OF APPLICANTS

1. Word of Mouth

Satisfied employees will recommend your company to their friends and relatives.
Advantages of hiring friends of employees
a. Saves you time, effort, and money in recruiting.
b. If the employee's performance is satisfactory, you could expect that the recommended friend will also become an effective employee.
c. The employee who recommends someone has a reputation to consider, so the employee will probably recommend someone who will meet the employee's expectations of an efficient employee.
d. Induction will be easier. Employees who are friends will work more co-operatively than strangers.
e. Turnover will be lower. Many new employees quit or are fired during their first few weeks on the job. The employee who did the recommending will use peer pressure to keep the friend from quitting and will help the friend achieve satisfactory performance.

Disadvantages of hiring friends of employees

a. The employee's friend might not be as good as your employee says.
b. Turnover could be higher. If either the employee or the friend plan to quit, you could lose both employees because of peer pressure. If you have a policy of hiring friends of employees, the responsibility for deciding whom to hire is yours and not your employees'. Check references. Don't just accept your employee's recommendation. He might not know his friend as well as he thinks he does.

What about hiring relatives of employees?—husbands, wives, sons, daughters, and so on. Many employers say no. But each situation should be considered on its own merits. For example, a married female employee may have commuting problems. If her husband became an employee, he could drive both to work in his car. However, if one of them is ill one day, you will probably have two absentees.

One unionized manufacturing company doing shift work had a policy of hiring relatives. The majority of the work force was hired on that basis. The company reasoned that, with so much of the family income coming from one source, the employees would never strike.

It might be all right to hire your employees' friends and relatives, but what about your own? The guidelines here should be: friends, maybe; relatives, no. Word of mouth can also be used by your suppliers, delivery people, letter carrier, banker, barber, and anyone else you talk to.

2. High Schools, Trade Schools, Colleges, Universities

You can contact the placement officer in person, by phone, or by mail. You can interview students at the institution or your place of business. One method is to screen applicants at the school, then invite suitable and interested applicants to your place of business. In the meantime, you can check references. Maintain good relationships with placement officers: they will recommend you and your company to their students.

3. Employment Agencies

Employment agencies can supply you with full-time or temporary employees. Temporaries are employees of the agency. You pay the temporary's salary or wages to the agency and the agency pays the employee. The agency deducts a fee before paying the employee.

After satisfactory performance, you might decide you want the temporary to be a full-time employee. The agency might not like losing a good employee to you, so be certain to read the fine print on any contract the agency wants you to sign.

Advantages of using an employment agency
a. The agency knows the job market—both the supply and the demand. It's the agency's full-time business.
b. The agency can save your time by interviewing and screening applicants.
c. The agency might be better than you are at screening, interviewing, and judging suitable applicants.
d. Only the agency knows that you need more employees. Your competitors and relatives won't find out.
e. The agency's fee might be cheaper than the cost of doing the recruiting yourself.
f. The agency might give a guarantee that the new employee will not quit for three or six months or whatever time period you agree on. If the employee quits during this period, the agency will return the fee you paid.

Disadvantages of using an employment agency
a. You might get an incompetent agency. You should talk directly to the agency person who will be assigned to your account. Assess this person as you would your own personnel manager.
b. The agency doesn't know your business as well as you do.
c. The agency works on commission. The sooner you hire someone, the sooner they get paid. Agencies have subtle and not-so-subtle ways of pressuring you to hire someone now, rather than wait for more applicants to be screened.
d. Agency fees could be more expensive than doing your own recruiting.

4. Canada Employment Centres

The Canada Employment Commission is a federal government employment agency which doesn't charge you a fee. Don't listen to all the complaints you've heard about this government department. Visit your local Canada Employment Centre. Find out what they can do for you. Many job seekers use the services of Canada Employment rather than a private employment agency. For some jobs, Canada Employment might be a good source— and the only source of applicants.

5. Unsolicited applications

Walk in, phone in, write in. Some applicants speculate and apply directly, hoping that you might need someone. Depending on the person's motivation and qualifications, this might be a good source of employees. If you can't employ the person now, you can keep the application on file. Later, a phone call to this person could save you a lot of time and effort in recruiting.

Always be courteous to applicants, especially when the answer is "no." Every applicant can spread goodwill or ill will about you. Word-of-mouth advertising is probably more believable than any other source of communication.

6. Advertising

Advertising in local newspapers usually attracts many applicants. Unemployed persons and those not satisfied with their jobs read the job ads every day. You can also use trade magazines, weekly community newspapers, and supermarket notice boards.

Here is a suggestion for minimizing the large number of un-qualified applicants who reply to job ads: use an ad big enough to tell your story. If you want to save money, consider your time and not the cost of the ad. A large ad will attract readership. The full story on the qualifications needed should screen out undesirable and unqualified persons. Consider your ad to be successful if it attracts a few qualified persons rather than a large number of unqualified or undesirable applicants. When you are advertising, be certain to obey all federal and provincial regulations. Exhibit 2-5 is a copy of the Ontario "Guidelines Respecting Job Advertising."

Most media will also help you with your advertising. Exhibit 2-6 is a sample of a large ad.

Some employers use box numbers because:
1. They don't want anyone (employees, competitors, friends and relatives) to know they have job vacancies.
2. They don't want applicants phoning or calling in person.
3. They don't have to say "no" to those they don't want to interview.

Should you use box numbers? Many job seekers have negative feelings when writing to box numbers. They wonder why the employer doesn't identify himself. The applicant is also asked to reveal personal information without knowing who is getting this information. How does the applicant know you won't check with the present employer? The most qualified persons probably won't answer ads with box numbers. Those who answer are probably unemployed, about to become unemployed, or simply unhappy with their present job. Some employers put this statement in their ad: "Our employees know of this ad." They hope this line will remove some of the suspicion about why a box number is being used.

7. Unions

In some industries the union hiring hall is a compulsory employment agency. A phone call to the union office saves the employer's time and effort in recruiting employees, but the employer also has to take whoever the union sends over.

Exhibit 2-5

Guidelines Respecting Job Advertising

Recent amendments to the Ontario Human Rights Code have consolidated into the Code the provisions of the Women's Equal Employment Opportunity Act.

This means that the Human Rights Code now prohibits discrimination on the basis of sex and marital status in addition to race, creed, colour, age, nationality, ancestry or place of origin.

In accordance with the new provisions, the following guidelines will serve to define for advertisers, newspapers and other publications the application of the advertising provisions as they relate to sex and marital status.

The intent of these provisions is to insure that no barriers exist—either real or implied—to discourage persons of either sex from seeking jobs for which they would be qualified and would be willing to perform.

GENERAL GUIDELINES

The Code includes advertising prohibitions which state that advertisers shall not place and publications shall not print advertisements limiting a position, either directly or indirectly, to a person on any of the grounds specified above in the Code.

cont'd

Exceptions

a. where sex or marital status is a *bona fide occupational qualification* and the employer has applied to the Commission and has been granted an EXEMPTION for the particular job (i.e. where it has been established that a particular sex or marital status is necessary to the actual performance of the job).
b. exclusively religious, philanthropic, educational, fraternal or social organizations not operated for private profit, where race, creed, colour, age, sex, marital status, nationality, ancestry or place of origin is a bona fide occupational qualification.

Confirmation of an exemption

Advertisers who have been granted an exemption by the Commission on the grounds of a *bona fide* occupational qualification will be assigned a reference number. In case of enquiry, we suggest that newspapers and other publications record the reference code number. Such exemptions are not automatic, but may be granted upon written request from employers at the discretion of the Commission. In order to clarify to the public that an exemption has been granted, it would be in the interest of both the publisher and advertiser to include in any advertisement for an exempted job the phrase "Human Rts. Comm. approv'd". If desired, the exemption reference number may be included.

c. domestics in a single family residence are automatically exempt.

The exemption previously operative under the Women's Equal Employment Opportunity Act to those employers of less than 6 employees is NO LONGER IN EFFECT.

Out-of-Province Advertisers: Advertisements placed by advertisers from outside the Province of Ontario are subject to the provisions of this legislation.

Publishers Share Responsibility With Advertisers for Any Breach of These Provisions

HELP WANTED CLASSIFICATIONS

The intent of the legislation is that a neutral, integrated column

cont'd

shall be used, or any alternative system which meets the intent of the legislation. Classifications and/or column headings which denote or may denote a preference (e.g. "Jobs of Interest to . . .") for one sex only are prohibited.

Examples of acceptable classifications are as follows:
a. Occupational Groupings: e.g. Automotive, Clerical, Domestic, Factory, Hospital, Hotel, Legal, Office, Professional, Restaurant, Sales, Skilled, Teachers, Technical, Unskilled, etc.
b. Alphabetical Listing by Job Title: e.g. Accountant to X-Ray Technician. Suggested column headings:

Help Wanted   Job Availabilities
Job Vacancies   Employment Opportunities

Employment Agency Listings

Job listings by employment agencies and/or management consultants are bound by the same policy as applies to Help Wanted Columns (i.e. must not be separated according to sex).

INDIVIDUAL ADVERTISEMENTS

Content

Individual advertisements must not imply any restriction or preference on the basis of sex or marital status or any of the other grounds specified in the code. This includes any descriptive wording (e.g. "housewives"), symbol, or representation (e.g. illustration) of a particular sex.

Exceptions to the above policy apply only where an exemption has been granted on the grounds of sex or marital status.

Use of a personal pronoun indicating gender (e.g. he, she) in the wording of advertisements is NOT acceptable. Alternate words such as the candidate, the person, the applicant, etc., is recommended.

Job Titles

In general, job titles will comply with the Code if they are NEUTRAL with regard to sex and marital status. The TEST of a NEUTRAL JOB TITLE is that it WOULD NOT DISCOURAGE QUALIFIED MALE OR FEMALE APPLICANTS.

The title should clearly DESCRIBE THE JOB—NOT THE GENDER OF THE PERSON DOING THE JOB. Wherever pos-

cont'd

sible, job titles ending with the suffix "man" or "woman" should be replaced with neutral descriptions such as:

person	agent	operator
worker	representative	attendant
helper	assistant	technician

Where there is doubt as to the neutrality of a job title and/or it is not possible to determine a suitable alternative, the use of any of the following techniques will indicate that no sex preference is intended:

a. double title which includes both genders: e.g. waiter/ waitress, foreman/woman, barmaid/man,
b. adding the words "male or female", or "men or women" following the job title; e.g. draftsman—male or female.

Reference Guide for Job Titles

A list of suggested neutral job titles has been prepared which may serve as a useful guide for newspapers and other publications. Copies of this reference guide are available, on request, from the Human Rights Commission, Ontario Ministry of Labour, 400 University Av., Toronto M7A 1T7. Phone 965-3841.

Source: Ontario Human Rights Commission.

RESUMES

A resumé is a summary of an applicant's education, work (or business) experience, and personal data. The resumé usually says good things about the applicant because it was prepared by the applicant. Some applicants submit resumés; some do not, especially for lower-level jobs.

Asking an applicant to submit a resumé has several advantages. First, most resumés can be read in two minutes. This is a fast way of screening applicants. You could use an application form as a substitute, but most applicants hate filling out application forms and resumés can be read faster. Second, if you get the resumé before the interview, you can be better prepared for planning your interview strategy. Third, in addition to the content, the resumé might tell you something else: whether the applicant is businesslike, organized, analytical, neat. However, the resumé could have been prepared by someone else.

Exhibit 2-6
Job Advertisement

Secretary

Skills needed: Typing 50 w.p.m. Dictation 90 w.p.m. Perfect in spelling and punctuation. Must be able to operate IBM word-processing equipment (transcribing and typing) without instruction. Must have Grade 12 (or equivalent) English skills in speaking, writing, and reading.

Will also be responsible for maintaining the Pendaflex filing system, operating the Xerox photocopier, the postage metre and coffee machine, telephone calls from both outside and inside the company, screening incoming mail and directing it to the appropriate department or person. Must be able to establish and maintain effective business relationships with employees.

Approximately 50% of time will be spent on dictation and typing and 50% on other office duties.

Working conditions: modern office in older-type building, 6 male and female employees of all ages in office and 30 other persons in other departments.

Hours 8:30 AM to 4:30 PM Monday to Friday. Must be punctual. Free parking. Bus stop 1 block away.

Restaurant (not licensed) within 10 minute walk. Industrial area. No shopping.

Salary: competitive and negotiable.

Reason for vacancy: present secretary getting married and moving out of town.

Starting date: within 2 to 4 weeks.

Reply in writing to: Ms. Susan Jones, Office Manager, ABC Co., 123 Anywhere St., Industrial Town Z1G 6E9.

APPLICATION FORMS

Ask yourself these questions when designing an application form:
1. What information do I need about an applicant before I make my decision to hire or not to hire?
2. Why do I need this information?
3. What information do I need for record purposes after the application is hired?
4. Why do I need this information?
5. Does this information contravene any government guidelines?

See Exhibit 2-7 for the Ontario "Human Rights In Employment." Exhibit 2-8 is an Application Form Worksheet. Use this form to make a list of the information you would like to have about a job applicant. The list will vary with the job position. Most small organizations use only one type of application form for all job categories. If you do the same, you will have to make your list all-inclusive.

Here are some suggestions: name, address, telephone, date of birth, marital status, dependents, next of kin, education, skills, career goals, references, languages (spoken and written), health, disabilities, convictions (other than minor traffic offence), driver's licence, bondable, debts, homeowner or tenant, work or business experience, hobbies or special interests.

In the second column of the Worksheet, write the reason why you want this information. You don't have to show a reason for the more obvious items such as name and address. But what about date of birth? The Human Rights Code says you cannot discriminate because of age, but you need the birthdate for pension purposes and so you won't hire minors. The application form you use should be tailored to your specific needs. Think of the time and expense in designing and producing the form as an investment in recruiting suitable employees.

In addition to being useful to you, the application form should be attractive to the applicant. You should want the job seeker to feel positive about your organization. Exhibit 2-9 is an example of a short application form which can be used for jobs where a minimum of information is needed. Exhibit 2-10 is an example of a comprehensive form which can be used when more information is needed. For verification, show your proposed application form to your provincial Human Rights Commission and ask for their advice and approval.

Exhibit 2-7

Human Rights in Employment
A Guide for Employers, Employees, and Employment Agencies

Contents

Hiring—questions on application forms and in interviews
1. *The Code and the Employer*
2. *Job Advertising (for employers and newspapers)*
3. *Advertising for 'Canadian Experience'*
4. *Job Orders to Employment Agencies*
5. *Immigration's Consequences*
6. *What Age Discrimination Means*
7. *Obtaining an Exemption (regarding age, sex and marital status)*
8. *Affirmative Action (corrective employment policies)*
9. *Complaint Procedure*

Background Information
10. *Section 4 of the Ontario Human Rights Code*
11. *The Code and the Ontario Human Rights Commission*

1. The Code and the Employer

The provisions of the Ontario Human Rights Code are intended to promote equal employment opportunities for all members of the labour force irrespective of race, religion, sex, nationality and age. Since merit transcends the boundaries of such irrelevant criteria, the employer is free to advertise, hire, screen or retain employees who are most capable of performing the job. The employer is free to define objectively valid qualifications necessary and relevant for satisfactory job performance, but once established they must apply equally to all applicants. The Code does not shield employees who are demonstrably incompetent or inadequate in their work.

**2. Job Advertising Under the Human Rights Code
(for employers and newspapers)**

The Human Rights Code prohibits discriminatory job advertising on all the prohibited grounds of discrimination listed in the Code. This applies both to the advertiser and to the newspaper. The newest of these grounds, and hence the most in need of stressing in the interests of public awareness, are age, sex and marital status.

Source: Ontario Human Rights Commission.

cont'd

No job advertisement may specify an upper age limit below the age of 65.

The intent of the provisions regarding job advertising and sex and marital status is to ensure that no barriers exist, either real or implied, to discourage persons of either sex, or of any marital status, from seeking jobs for which they believe themselves qualified.

In pursuit of this objective, all newspapers now have integrated 'help wanted' columns in place of the former division by male and female. Classified advertisements may be divided into occupational groupings, e.g. automotive, clerical, factory, office, professional, sales, technical, unskilled.

Individual advertisements must avoid wording which would indicate a preference for, or an expectation regarding, one sex rather than the other. Therefore the words "he" and "she" are replaced by such neutral words as the candidate, the person, or the applicant.

Job titles should be such as would not discourage qualified male or female applicants. Job titles describe the job, not the gender of the person doing the job. Titles ending in 'man' or 'woman' should be replaced by such words as agent, operator, worker, assistant, representative.

Where there is a difficulty, double titles can be used, e.g. waiter/waitress, foreman/woman, or the words 'male or female' can be added after the job title, e.g. draftsman—male or female.

3. Advertising for 'Canadian Experience'

The Commission has advised all newspaper publishers of its concern to eliminate the use of the phrase 'Canadian experience', with the co-operation of the press, because the phrase is often used to discriminate against immigrants and thus to circumvent hiring on the basis of merit.

Even when there is no discriminatory intent, the phrase has the effect of discouraging immigrants from applying for jobs for which they feel qualified.

The Commission urges employers to substitute a more precise and hence meaningful description of the desired job requirements, and asserts its belief that providing such accurate, job-related requirements will save the time of the employer as well as of job applicants.

The Commission urges job candidates who may be deterred by any advertisements which do ask for 'Canadian experience'

cont'd

to interpret the phrase in specific terms and apply for the job if they feel they are qualified. If an unsuccessful job applicant seeks to lodge a complaint with the Commission in the belief that he or she was discriminated against on the ground of nationality, and if the advertisement for the job asked for 'Canadian experience', the Commission will process the complaint.

4. Job Orders to Employment Agencies

It is unlawful for any employer to seek to place a job order, or for an employment agency to accept a job order, which limits applicants on the basis of race, creed, colour, age, sex, marital status, nationality, ancestry or place or origin.
(See also 'Immigration's Consequences'.)

5. Immigration's Consequences

1. A desire to discriminate is sometimes disguised by alleging that a job candidate who is a recent immigrant lacks 'Canadian experience'. Because this 'requirement' can lead to abuse, a job-seeker who receives this reply should examine its validity. If he or she has reason to believe it is not valid, he or she should discuss it with the Commission, which is prepared to establish, by investigation, the factors involved in the job which allegedly necessitate the requirement and to evaluate those factors in terms of discriminatory intent.
2. The federal immigration law specifies who is and who is not eligible to work in Canada. Hence it is permissible for an employer to ask the following question on an application form:
   'Are you legally entitled to work in Canada? Those so entitled are Canadian citizens, landed immigrants or holders of a valid work permit.'

An employer may ask for documentary proof of eligibility to work in Canada after hiring.

6. What Age Discrimination Means

An employee may not be refused employment or terminated simply because he or she has reached an age over 40 or under 65.
The Code does not confer any special privileges upon persons aged 40 to 65 in the workplace. It ensures equal opportunity in employment regardless of age. Job advertisements

cont'd

may not circumvent the prohibition against a stated upper age limit below 65 by such phrases as 'recent graduate'.

7. Obtaining an Exemption
(regarding age, sex and marital status)

The Code has a number of clauses identified as 'exceptions'; the relevant ones here are those which permit employers to apply in writing for an exemption from the provisions regarding age, sex and marital status, in order to advertise for one sex only, or to specify marital status or an age bracket below 65. The investigation which follows upon the application takes as its criterion whether the requested limitation truly represents a bona fide occupational qualification and requirement. Exemptions are not granted automatically but at the discretion of the Commission. (There is a further exception, section 4(7), with respect to religious, philanthropic, educational, fraternal or social organizations.)

Non-discrimination on the basis of age, sex and marital status is applied by law to employee benefit plans. It is administered by the Employment Standards Branch of the Ministry of Labour.

8. Affirmative Action   (corrective employment policies)

Discrimination is sometimes unconsciously "built into" a company's hiring and promotion practices even if management positively wishes to follow the principles of the Human Rights Code. These practices can be left over from an earlier period when their purpose was indeed discriminatory. When such practices are followed as part of the company's hiring procedures, then, even if personnel officers act on the merit principle, they may still be excluding particular ethnic or racial groups, or women. In part this is because past exclusion of certain groups in our society from entry or promotion opportunities has resulted in their lacking the necessary education, training, job attitude or general motivation.

In such situations the achieving of true equality may require that the merit principle be suspended, under carefully controlled and supervised conditions. Section 6a of the Human Rights Code provides for this. The intention is that suspensions of the merit principle will be treated as exceptional, and will be approved only after the Commission has carefully examined the particular situation.

cont'd

The Commission encourages companies to discover for themselves if their personnel practices are discriminatory in their neutral application and, if they are, to introduce positive corrective measures which have been approved by the Commission under section 6a.

This section was added to the Code in 1972 to permit such corrective, compensatory employment programs, usually termed affirmative action programs. Section 6a allows employers to apply to the Commission for an exception in their hiring practices so that they may favour a particular group, thus suspending in part the merit principle.

The Commission is ready to explain and assist in carrying out an affirmative action policy. Both the employer and the community benefit from such policies. The employer gains a valuable new source of manpower, including present employees whose abilities may not be fully tapped because of old promotion practices.

Note that section 6a does not come into play where efforts are made to *expand* the pool of potential job applicants by advertising more widely, by providing on-the-job training, etc. That is because the merit principle still determines the final selection of the successful applicant. The Commission encourages such practices apart from section 6a in order to promote such expansion.

9. Complaint Procedure
(what employers should know)

The Code provides that any person who feels victimized by discrimination within the terms set by the Code may lodge a complaint with the Commission. It is incumbent upon the Commission to investigate a complaint, once filed, to establish if it can be substantiated, and to seek to resolve the matter through a conciliation settlement. The Code also provides for the Commission initiating a complaint.

The employer plays a necessary role in this process. The employer should therefore be acquainted with the nature of the complaint-handling process. If the investigation concludes that the complaint is substantiated, the Commission will seek to rectify the situation. If the investigation concludes that the complaint is not well-founded, the Commission will attempt to correct the complainant's perception of discrimination and explain the real circumstances in the matter.

If the complaint cannot be resolved it is submitted to the

cont'd

Human Rights Commissioners. They may recommend to the Minister of Labour that a public Board of Inquiry be appointed to hold hearings and take evidence regarding the complaint and to make recommendations for its resolution. Those recommendations have the force of law. The Commissioners may recommend to the Minister of Labour that a Board of Inquiry not be held, which has the effect of dismissing the complaint.

10. Section 4 of the Human Rights Code

The employment provisions in section 4 of the Code are based on the principle of merit employment. This means that people are not excluded from employment opportunities by irrelevant criteria such as race, religion, nationality, sex, marital status or age. The Code provides that hiring, training, promotion, seniority lists, transfer, probationary status and its duration, and any 'terms and conditions of employment' are to be established solely on the basis of ability, experience and individual qualities.

The prohibitions of the Code apply specifically to trade unions and self-governing professions as well as to employers.

11. The Code and the Ontario Human Rights Commission

The Ontario Human Rights Commission, a part of the Ontario Provincial Government, has the objective of ensuring equal opportunity, free of discrimination, for all people living and working in Ontario. The Commission administers the Ontario Human Rights Code, passed in 1962, which prohibits discrimination on the basis of race, creed, colour, sex, marital status, nationality, ancestry, place of origin and age (40 to 65).

The Code applies in the areas of employment—including membership in unions and professional associations—housing, public accommodation (which means access to facilities and services available to the public), and related advertising.

To achieve this objective the Commission investigates and conciliates complaints of discrimination, maintains a continuing campaign of public education, works at the community level to resolve group friction and tension situations, and conducts research into community problems and changing social attitudes.

The Code relies for its ultimate effectiveness on public awareness and support from all citizens and residents of Ontario, native-born and newcomers.

cont'd

The Commission urges all citizens and residents to regard the following as their responsibilities:

Become acquainted with the Ontario Human Rights Code and know the provisions that pertain to your rights and responsibilities in employment.

Report to the Ontario Human Rights Commission any experienced or observed act of discrimination, or advise the victim of the possibility of lodging a complaint, or explain the Code and the Commission's work to the parties involved and those responsible for carrying out personnel functions.

If you are an employer, post the 'Declaration of Management Policy' card prominently in your place of business. This will indicate to employees and public alike that you support the principles of the Code.

When recruiting new employees, see that advertisements and job orders comply with the Code. Do not depend on newspapers or employment agencies to do the job for you.

If you have questions or suggestions regarding human rights in employment contact the Commission office nearest you.

OBJECTIVE OF THE CODE

It is public policy in Ontario that every person is free and equal in dignity and rights without regard to race, creed, colour, age, sex, marital status, nationality, ancestry or place of origin.
The aim of Ontario's Human Rights Code is to create at the community level a climate of understanding and mutual respect, in which all our people, of whatever racial, religious or cultural background—new Canadians no less than native born—will be made to feel that all are equal in dignity and rights, that each is a part of the whole Canadian community, and that each has a rich contribution to make to the development and well being of our province and nation. Few will disagree that this is a prerequisite for the building of a truly healthy Canadianism.

cont'd

Exhibit 2-7 (cont'd)

Hiring—Questions on Application Forms and in Interviews
Any inquiry is forbidden w information as to race, cr violation of the Ontario Hum

Category	Approved	
1. Name	Name used if previously employed under different name	Pr been changed by court order or otherwise
2. Address	Place and duration of current and previous address in Canada	Foreign address, indicating national origin
3. Birthplace, nationality, ancestry, place of origin		a. Birth or baptismal certificate Birth certificate b. Place of birth c. Place of birth of parents, grandparents or spouse d. Any inquiry into national origin
4. Age, sex and marital status	May be asked but may not be used to discriminate	Any personnel actions which suggest that age, sex or marital status have been an influence
5. Race or colour	Height and weight *only* if job-related	Race, colour, complexion, colour of eyes, colour of hair

cont'd

Exhibit 2-7 (cont'd)

6. Photograph	Request for photograph or taking of a photograph	Photograph for identification purposes
7. Religion, creed	a. Any inquiry to identify religious denomination or customs b. Clergyman's recommendation or reference (Note: an employer may not state "This is a Protestant *or* Catholic *or* Jewish organization"	Any special religious holidays for which employee will require leave of absence
8. Citizenship	(For questions regarding legal eligibility to work in Canada, see 'Immigration's Consequences') a. Whether a Canadian citizen or British subject b. If native-born or naturalized c. Date citizenship received d. Proof of citizenship e. Citizenship status of parents or spouse f. Any inquiry into citizenship status which would tend to divulge applicant's nationality, ancestry, or place of origin	

9. Education	a. Academic, professional, or vocational secondary and post-secondary schools attended b. Language skills, i.e. reading and writing of foreign languages	a. Elementary school: name and location b. Nationality, racial or religious affiliation of a school c. What mother tongue is d. How foreign language ability acquired	
10. Relatives		a. Name and address of closest relative b. Any inquiry about a relative which cannot be asked of a job applicant	Name and address of person to be notified in case of emergency
11. Membership in organizations	Any inquiry into membership organizations, with proviso: "Do not list clubs or organizations of a religious, racial, or national character"	a. All clubs or organizations where membership is held b. Any specific inquiry into clubs and organizations which would indicate race, creed, colour, nationality, ancestry or place of origin	
12. Work schedule	Willingness to work required work schedule	Willingness to work on any particular religious holiday	When leave of absence might be required for observance of religious holidays
13. Military service	Canadian military service	All military service	

Exhibit 2-8

Application Form Worksheet

What information is needed?	Why?	When? Before or after interview? Use B or A	Is this information legal? Yes or No

Exhibit 2-9
Short Application Form

A.B.C. Company

1. Name (please print) _____

2. Address _____

3. Phone: Business _____ Home _____

4. Position wanted _____

5. Permanent _____ Temporary _____ Part time _____

6. Part-time days and hours preferred _____

7. Qualifications (show skills)

   a. Education and training: _____

   _____

   _____

   b. Experience (show employers and names of your supervisors): _____

   _____

   _____

8. Marital status _____

9. Health (show disabilities) _____

10. What else would you like us to know about you? _____

   _____

11. Wage or salary expected: $_____

12. Are you legally entitled to work in Canada? _____

13. Signature _____ Date _____

Exhibit 2-10
Long Application Form

A.B.C. Company

Date: _____

1. Position wanted: _____
2. Name (please print) _____ Mr. or Ms. _____
3. Address _____
4. Phone: Business _____ Home _____
5. Social Insurance Number _____
6. Are you legally entitled to work in Canada? _____
7. What languages do you
   a. Speak _____
   b. Write _____
   c. Read _____
8. Wages or salary expected: _____
9. When can you start work? _____
10. Have you ever been bonded? _____ Refused bond? _____
11. What disabilities do you have that might interfere with your ability to do your work? _____
12. How will you get to work? _____
13. Have you ever been convicted of other than a minor traffic offence? _____
14. What job injuries have you had? _____
15. Have you ever applied for Workmen's Compensation? _____
16. How many days were you absent in the last 12 months for
    a. Illness _____
    b. Other reasons _____
17. Marital status _____
18. Age (if under 18) _____
19. Goals or career objective _____

20. Why do you want this job? _____
21. What else would you like to tell us about yourself? _____

22. I certify that the information I have written is true and complete. I understand that a false statement will disqualify me from employment or will cause my dismissal.

Signature _____ Date _____

Education

Type of School	Name and location	Dates Attended From To	Course Studied	Grade Completed, Diploma, or Degree
Secondary				
Trade or technical				
Business or commercial				
College or university				
Other (specify)				

Certificates, licences, professional qualifications: _____

Special skills (typing, shorthand, business machines, computers): _____
_____

Employment History

(Put most recent employer first)
1. Present employer and address: _____
_____

cont'd

Exhibit 2-10 (cont'd)

Job title and duties: _____

Date of employment: From _____

Wages or salary: $ _____ Phone: _____ May we contact? _____

Supervisor: _____

Reason for wanting to leave: _____

2. Previous employer and address: _____

Job title and duties: _____

Dates of employment: From _____ To _____

Wages or salary: $ _____ Phone: _____ May we contact? _____

Supervisor: _____

Reason for leaving: _____

3. Previous employer and address: _____

Job title and duties: _____

Dates of employment: From _____ To _____

Wages or salary: $ _____ Phone: _____ May we contact? _____

Supervisor: _____

Reason for leaving: _____

4. Canadian Military Service

Dates: From _____ To _____

Duties and responsibilities: _____

Training and skills: _____

Rank on discharge _____ Type of Discharge _____

References _____
_____
_____

SCREENING

A screen is a negative device. Its purpose is to keep things out rather than to let things in. If we didn't have to keep things out we wouldn't need a screen. It's the same with job applicants. Screening is the process of preventing undesirable applicants from becoming employees.

Use your job specifications to determine the qualifications you want in an applicant. You should also know what characteristics you don't want. For example, an applicant may have all the desired qualifications as well as some undesirable characteristics. Remember, you are hiring the whole person, not just the part or parts you want.

Screening is a subjective human process, so everyone makes mistakes—both in letting undesirables in and in keeping good applicants out. The decision to eliminate some applicants can be easily made; for others, the decision is more difficult.

What should you do when you have doubts?
1. Carefully compare the job specifications with the applicant's qualifications. Try to be objective. Try to make a rational rather than an emotional decision.
2. Be realistic. The ideal applicant is rare. You will have to accept applicants with some undesirable qualifications, especially if there is a shortage of desirable applicants.
3. If you still have doubts, say "No." You might be rejecting a potentially good employee, but you are preventing a problem. Many managers say that most of their on-the-job problems are people problems—so why should you hire a problem?

The Human Rights Code prohibits discrimination on the grounds of race, creed, colour, age, sex, marital status, nationality, ancestry, or place of origin. You don't have to tell applicants why they were rejected. But if you do give a reason, be certain that you are complying with the Human Rights Code. However, despite the best laws in the country, there will always be discrimination based on personal feelings and what our experience has taught us. Experience is a great teacher, but it can also close our mind to opportunities.

For example, answer these questions:
1. What is my attitude toward women in business, especially for supervisory and management positions?
2. What do I think of young people and their attitudes, expectations, behaviour, alienation, and lifestyles?

3. What should I do about older applicants, especially those people over 40?
4. Should I hire new Canadians who have good work habits, but are culturally different?
5. What is my attitude toward the physically and mentally handicapped?
6. Would I hire persons who tend to be passed over by other employers (ex-convicts, welfare recipients, chronically unemployed)?
7. Do your attitudes comply with the Human Rights Code?

You can hire these people for humanitarian reasons, but you can also hire them for business reasons.

Data Sheet

Because your organization might be unknown to job applicants, you should prepare a one- or two-page summary of the following:
1. Nature of the business. Your products or services, market served.
2. Number of employees and the types of jobs they have.
3. Company history and prospects.

This should be a fact sheet, not a piece of propaganda. This data sheet can be mailed to applicants or given to applicants who apply in person. This information summary can save you the time of explaining what your organization does as well as screen out applicants who are not interested in working for you.

3

RECRUITING: INTERVIEWS, REFERENCES, TESTS

You've decided what kind of person you want to hire and how to go about finding that person. Now you have to pick that person from a group of applicants. First, you have to get to know the applicants better. This chapter describes the techniques for getting to know your applicants so you can find out which one best suits your needs.

INTERVIEWING

Interviewing is a skill that can be learned. It is a skill that all managers and supervisors should learn. Interviewing skills can be used for job interviews, orientation, problem solving, counselling, performance appraisal, complaints, and discipline. An employment interview has two purposes: you evaluate the applicant and the applicant evaluates you, the job, and the organization.

One of the greatest drawbacks to the interview is that it is subjective and depends on the personal interpretation of the interviewer, who is quite likely to be inconsistent from interview to interview. As a matter of interest, it has been proven that interviewers have different interpretations and judgements at different times. Also, the information obtained from interviews is not easy to record or quantify. Effective interviewing requires emotional maturity, social adeptness, and perception of personality, attitudes, and motivation. An interviewer has to know how to collect facts systematically and to assess their significance.

When an interview is conducted with the purpose of hiring, the interviewer should be reasonably sure that the interviewee will be successful at the job. To be reasonably sure, the interviewer must carefully match the applicant's qualifications against the job requirements. The interviewer must be sure that the person can do the job and that the person has the necessary skills, ability, and physical and intellectual characteristics required. In addition, the interviewer must evaluate the applicant's work habits, motivation, and emotional control before deciding whether the applicant can perform the job effectively. That is, what a person has done and why that person has done it determine behavioural patterns which will probably be repeated. You should not expect that people will change their personalities and behaviours when they come to work for you.

The information you need is on the application form. Seven "adjustment areas" should be investigated and they form the pattern for the interview—work history, education, family, social, economic, health, and hobbies.

Work history is perhaps the most important adjustment area because it is the area most closely related to the person's present behaviour pattern and to the position applied for. The interviewer must determine the pattern of jobs which indicates the applicant's stability. For example, if the applicant has held one type of job, has not made many changes from one company to another, this would indicate a stable character. If, on the other hand, a person seems to be a job hopper, this is a danger sign and might indicate instability. Reasons for leaving a job, the number of positions held, and the time spent in each one are valuable clues, but should not be judged on face value alone. It sometimes happens that the reasons for changing are always the same; for example, perhaps the applicant always feels unfairly treated by employers. The chances are that the applicant will probably feel the same way about a new employer. The level of job will show whether progress has been made within a company or from one firm to another. This progress (or lack of it) shows the interviewer the applicant's level of ambition and motivation.

Educational background should be matched with the demands of the job. It is essential to distinguish between the applicant's knowledge gained and ability to perform. The interviewer should examine formal and informal training, which could include night and correspondence courses, reading, contact in similar work, and the applicant's current interests. The important thing is to find out the person's attitude toward school: it can indicate behaviour patterns. For example, if the candidate objected to school discipline or had difficulty adjusting to it, the chances are the applicant will have difficulty adjusting to the discipline required by an effective manager. The applicant's extracurricular activities at school suggest social skills and capacity for leadership. Also, determining the applicant's stability in persisting with one course and finishing it, instead of jumping around, will carry over as a behavioural pattern in the job experience. General attitude toward teachers and other students will give clues to maturity on the job and how the applicant will fit in with co-workers. It is quite safe to say that the same pattern established continues from school to job and from job to job.

Family background covers both parental family and marital family. The parental family influences the way the candidate gets on at school and both family and school influence the way the applicant gets on at work. From the socio-economic development of the applicant's family the interviewer can learn a good deal about the applicant's job-level expectations.

The way a candidate handles personal finances gives some clue of practical judgement. Past earnings are a rough guide to ability in normal times. A wide variation between past earnings and present salary, or the salary of the job under consideration, might indicate either deterioration of ability or unrealistic ambition. A person's economic stability is indicated by systematic savings, intelligent insurance plans, and a good credit rating. If the applicant spends beyond his or her means and is constantly in debt, this would indicate impulsiveness and lack of judgement.

Medical examination is becoming the normal trend of many organizations. Whether or not it is done formally with a doctor, the interviewer is responsible for a general check of an applicant's physical condition against work demands and for spotting clues to emotional maladjustment in relation to the job.

Hobbies can reveal much about a candidate's attitude, stability, and maturity. The chances are that a person who works hard at hobbies related to the job will also work hard at the job. More important, hobbies show what the candidate likes to do.

The opening minutes of an interview can be critical. Applicant and interviewer are both creating and receiving important first impressions. Both are assessing each other's appearance, manner, and voice. The interviewer's manner and voice must project to the applicant a person whom the applicant can warm to and trust. Most candidates have a natural tendency to feel nervous and tense at the beginning of an interview and the responsibility for relieving this tension rests with the interviewer. The interviewer's own complete relaxation is one of the best methods of relaxing the candidate. The interviewer must establish a rapport with the candidate in order for the latter to confide in an uninhibited manner. This feeling is not something that the interviewer establishes at the beginning and then turns off, but is maintained through a conscious ongoing activity. Although the interviewer must put the applicant at ease, the interviewer's manner should never be forced or false. Good human relations are the basis of this rapport. A simple smile, genuine interest, intelligent listening, and sincerity are the keys to establishing this type of relationship.

After preliminaries of introduction and sitting down are concluded, the interviewer should open the conversation with some appropriate remark directly related to the applicant. This shows the interviewee that the interviewer is familiar with the application and is acquainted with the applicant's background and experience. Some interviewing manuals state that continuous note taking during an interview, with the applicant's knowledge, is essential to the interviewer who seeks a detailed and accurate recall and evaluation. Personally, I prefer to waive this technique, as I find it distracting both to myself and probably to the applicant. However, I do ensure that all gaps and missing information in the application are obtained, whether by direct questions at the start of the interview or through questioning during the interview.

Nothing can be more frustrating for an interviewer than to have an applicant who will not talk. Sometimes I feel prospective applicants should attend a course on how to market themselves. However, a good interviewer can usually persuade the quietest candidate to talk by asking one question at a time (not multiple questions in one sentence), by asking questions which cannot be answered with just a "yes" or "no" (that is, ask open-ended questions so the candidate has to expand answers), by pausing after a candidate has finished answering, giving the candidate an opportunity to elaborate or clarify, by moving from one subject to another and controlling the interview to prevent any abrupt changes of pace or mood, by using vernacular familiar to the candidate, by showing complete interest, and by never implying criticism or overagreement with what is being said.

The way a question is phrased can elicit either the right or the wrong response. Sometimes, however, even the "desirable" wording will not produce the necessary information; for example,

"Which was your favourite subject in school?" instead of "You didn't obtain your senior matriculation. Didn't you like school?" When this occurs, the interviewer should ask a followup question, for example, "What else did you do?" (The problem of asking a question in order to receive an unbiased answer is one commonly shared with the consumer-market researcher.) There is no sense asking a question if the applicant only gives the answer thought to be what the interviewer expected.

Exhibit 3-1 is a list of interview questions. Select those questions that you think are appropriate and prepare additional questions that you think will be needed. During the interview, you don't have to follow your list rigidly: be flexible to suit the circumstances.

Persuading candidates to talk about themselves is an important part of interviewing; equally important is truly understanding what they say. Listening is a major skill of interviewing and, from my own experience, I would say 80% of the interview is devoted to listening. This only seems logical: since the purpose of the interview is to obtain information about the candidate, it would follow that the majority of the interviewer's time would be spent in listening.

The interviewer first listens to what is being said in an attempt to evaluate the applicant's words. Listening intelligently leads on to further and deeper questions; facts are uncovered which otherwise might be obscured behind generalities. Listening also reveals not only facts, but also the emotion or feeling which surrounds the fact. Listening to the emotional overtones will often reveal a false note of an uneasiness which can be a prelude to evasion. The ability to sense the inner meaning of a candidate's statement is a very personal skill: something of a sixth sense is required in order to detect such readings.

An effective interview, skillfully handled, can reveal the candidate not only to the interviewer but also to the candidate. This sort of revelation happens rarely, although every interviewer should be prepared for the possibility because it could be traumatic; it is the interviewer's job to guide the interviewee to an understanding of what is being revealed. Speaking dramatically (and theoretically), an interview can have a cathartic effect for some applicants, since they are able to talk to someone without receiving criticism or blame. The interviewer is in turn able to evaluate the applicant's aptitude and interpersonal skills.

Controlling an interview can be a very tricky task. The candidate must be steered to provide the necessary information during

Exhibit 3-1
Suggested Interview Questions

Note: *Refer to the Human Rights Code for guidelines on what you may ask. Tell the applicant, "It is my intention to comply with the Human Rights Code. Any deviation is a mistake and is not intentional."*

1. How did you get your last job?
2. What are your duties and responsibilities?
3. How did the company treat you?
4. What did you learn from your previous jobs?
5. Which job did you like the most? Why?
6. Which job did you like the least? Why?
7. Do you like routine work? Why?
8. Would you prefer to work for a large or small organization? Why?
9. What type of supervisor do you prefer? Why?
10. What determines a person's progress in a company?
11. Do you want a permanent job or a temporary job? Why?
12. Do you prefer working in a group or team or by yourself? Why?
13. Do you like regular or flexible hours? Why?
14. If you could pick any job, which one would you choose? Why?
15. Where do you expect to be in 5 years? Why?
16. What is your best characteristic?
17. What are your strengths?
18. What are your weaknesses?
19. What do you do to keep up to date in your work?
20. Which types of people do you like working with? Why?
21. Which types of people do you not like working with? Why?
22. Why did you leave your previous jobs?
23. Why do you want to leave your present job?
24. May we contact your former employers?
25. May we contact your present employer?
26. Everyone makes mistakes. What types of mistakes do you make?
27. What have you learned from these mistakes?
28. What experience have you had in supervising people?
29. What qualifications do you have for the job you're applying for?
30. What are your career plans?
31. What experience have you had in planning? Organizing? Problem solving? Decision making?

cont'd

32. What happens when you work under pressure?
33. What is an interesting job?
34. Do you prefer working with men or women? Why?
35. Do you prefer a male or female supervisor? Why?
36. If we hire you, what do you hope will happen during your first year?
37. What have you learned from your part-time jobs? Your summer jobs?
38. Would your previous employers rehire you? Why?
39. What skills (talents, knowledge) do you have that haven't been used on your jobs?
40. If you don't get this job, what will you do?
41. Other than money, what is important in a job?
42. Would you like to be a supervisor? Why?
43. No job or organization is perfect. What imperfections can you tolerate?
44. What do you think of competition within an organization?
45. What do you think of orders and instructions? Why?
46. What don't you like about other people? Why?
47. Why would you like to work for us?
48. Who do you know that works here?
49. What on-the-job accidents have you had?
50. Are you receiving compensation for a job injury?
51. What physical disabilities do you have?
52. How many days were you absent during the last 12 months?
53. Why were you absent?
54. Do you have a part-time job? Why?
55. Have you ever been unemployed? When? Why? For how long?
56. How many jobs have you applied for?
57. Has your pay ever been decreased? Why?
58. Have you ever been demoted?
59. What subjects did you like best at school? Why?
60. What subjects did you like least at school? Why?
61. What were your extracurricular activities? Why?
62. How important are a student's grades?
63. What percentage of your school expenses did you pay?
64. How did you earn the money?
65. Why did you go to trade school, college, university?
66. What are your plans for continuing your education?
67. Which teachers did you like the best? Why?
68. Which teachers did you not like? Why?
69. What is your marital status?

cont'd

70. Are you self-supporting?
71. What debts do you have?
72. What do you do with your spare time?
73. What illnesses or injuries have you had in the past year? (two years?)
74. Does your spouse work? Where?
75. What hobbies do you have?
76. What do you do on your holidays?
77. What do you do to keep healthy?
78. What do you think about drinking and drugs?
79. Have you ever been convicted of anything other than a minor traffic offence?
80. What do you do with your pay?
81. What do you do about saving money?
82. What do you think is a good investment for your savings?
83. Should the husband or wife manage the family's finances? Why?
84. What wages (salary) are you expecting? Why?
85. Have you ever been bonded? When? Why?
86. Would you be willing to be bonded? Why?
87. What method of transportation will you use to get to work?
88. Do you have other sources of income?
89. How many dependents do you have?

Add some questions that you would like to ask:
90. _____
91. _____
92. _____
93. _____

Here are three questions that you should ask every job applicant:
1. What do you know about our company? (or) What do you know about our industry?
2. Why do you want this job?
3. Why should we hire you?

The answer to the first question will show the applicant's interest in your company or type of business; if the applicant does not have any specific interest in your company or the industry you are in, this is an indication that the person would accept employment from anyone. That is, the applicant who has reasons for wanting to work for you is more likely to stay with your organization. The answer to the second question will show you the applicant's motivation. The answer to the third question will show you the qualifications that the applicant thinks he or she has.

cont'd

The employer has to answer these three questions:
1. Is the applicant interested in us?
2. Does the applicant have the motivation we're looking for?
3. Is the applicant qualified for the job?

the interview. The interviewer has predetermined the time allotments and knows how much time can be spent on each section. Occasionally, the interviewer must exercise real control by bringing back the applicant, tactfully but firmly, to areas avoided during the interview. Controlling the interview is especially necessary when the candidate is experienced and attempts to direct the interview.

If you decide that the applicant is qualified for the job, you can then answer questions. If you decide that the applicant isn't qualified, then don't waste your time or create false hopes by telling a lot about the job and the organization.

Closing an interview should be as consciously controlled by the interviewer as any other section. The close is often the time of unintended revelation. A candidate, feeling the hardest part is over, may unwittingly reveal more of the true self behind an image so carefully preserved throughout the interview.

If I have a fairly good idea that I am going to recommend a candidate, I will often close with something like, "Are there any questions you would like to ask me?" The reaction to this often helps illuminate the candidate's quality and understanding of what has been discussed during the interview. The close of the interview should again stress good human relations. It is usually the final words of an interview which are remembered longest. The candidate should be left knowing the next stage in recruitment or its timing.

Academic Achievement

When assessing an applicant's academic achievement at school, college, or university, should you be looking for "A," "B," or "C" grades?

Many business managers are of the opinion that a "C" student has a better personality and is more suitable for the practical business world than "A" or "B" students. What you have to determine is whether or not the "C" student could have achieved "A"s or "B"s but didn't. Some "C" students are more intelligent than those who achieve higher grades, but these "C" students were not willing to put forth the necessary effort.

Some intelligent "A" and "B" students achieve their high grades with a minimum of effort. Some "C" students have to work hard to achieve their relatively lower grade. But maybe that "C" student is the person you want in a job that requires someone with ambition, drive, and determination to succeed.

Some potential "A" students become "B" students because of the time spent on extracurricular activities: some of these extracurricular activities could have been more educational than formal classes. Further, these students may have been active in student organizations that provided learning experiences for social and leadership skills. These skills may be more important to an employer than high academic achievement. Other students may have had low grades because of their part-time jobs.

In evaluating a person's academic achievement, the employer has to decide:
1. How important are grades as a job specification?
2. What caused the student to have "A," "B," or "C" grades?
3. Did the student use good judgement in the use of time and effort for academic and non-academic activities?

Interviewer's Evaluation

The interviewer should make a written evaluation of the applicant immediately after the interview.

The interviewer can write comments about the person or complete an Evaluation Report Form. (See Exhibit 3-2 for an example.)

An Evaluation Report Form can be used in planning an interview. The Report also ensures that the evaluation will be complete and that the interviewer will make a decision on the suitability of the applicant.

Exhibit 3-2

Interviewer's Evaluation Report

(Confidential)

Job: _____

Applicant: _____

Interviewed by: _____ Date: _____

Check off or comment on the items you observed or found out. Do not guess at the other items: leave them blank. Not all

cont'd

items are relevant for every job. Your answer should be "yes" or "no." We cannot hire "maybe" or "not certain."
You can qualify your "yes" or "no" under "comments."

Evaluate the applicant on the following:

                                          Yes/No   Comments

1. Work experience necessary to perform the job satisfactorily.
2. Skills with machines, tools, equipment.
3. Skills with job procedures.
4. Experience with special projects.
5. Formal education.
6. Trade or vocational education.
7. Continuing education and training (off-the-job).
8. On-the-job training.
9. Will need training for this job.
10. Ability to get along with supervisor.
11. Ability to get along with fellow employees.
12. Ability to work as a member of a team or work group.
13. Applicant's comments of former supervisor.
14. Plans.
15. Attendance record.
16. Punctuality.
17. Safety record.
18. Health.
19. Physical strength to perform job.
20. Good work habits.
21. Supervisory experience.
22. Prefers to work alone.
23. Primarily interested in money.
24. Prefers non-financial rewards.
25. Likes the work.
26. Blames others.
27. Flexible. Can adjust to changes.
28. Has a part-time job.
29. Are off-the-job activities

cont'd

consistent with on-the-job
activities and personality?
30. Is appearance favourable?
31. Is applicant well mannered?
32. Does applicant have
self-confidence?
33. Ability to communicate orally.

Summary   *Comments*
34. Why does the applicant want
this job?
35. Does the applicant have
enough qualifications?
36. If hired, how long will the
applicant stay?
37. If hired, should the applicant
be put on probation?
38. If so, for how long?
39. Is the applicant worth training?
40. Other comments.
41. I recommend that the applicant
be hircd: (subject to
confirmation of information)

Signature: _____

CHECKING REFERENCES

Always ask the applicant for the names of references, even if
you don't plan to contact these references. By asking, you can
find out:
1. Does the applicant have references?
2. Does the applicant supply the names willingly or unwillingly?
3. Does the applicant supply the names of supervisors?

The applicant who gives you the names of persons other than
supervisors will only pick persons who will say good things
about the applicant. When you contact these references, you
will be able to determine some of the good characteristics of the
applicant. But if you contact anyone, it should be the supervisor.
And be certain to get the names of all of the supervisors the
applicant had at the same company. An employee who has had
more than one supervisor will only want to give you the name of
the person who will give favourable information.

Don't go too far back into a person's history. Supervisors of years ago may not remember the employee very well. The best you can do in these circumstances is to check the company's records for written data.

Always check references by telephone. Supervisors prefer to talk about a former employee rather than put comments into writing. A phone call also gets faster results. Long-distance calls should be made if necessary. The cost of a call is an investment in preventing a recruiting mistake. Be certain to tell the applicant that you plan to phone long distance to check references. Some applicants think that you won't want to spend money and use your time for checking.

Exhibit 3-3 is a suggested format you can use when phoning a supervisor or a personnel manager. Depending on the job to be filled, you might want to check an applicant's credit and criminal records.

Exhibit 3-3

Reference Checking of Former Employer

1. Person to be phoned: _____ Phone: _____
2. Company: _____
3. Department, position, title: _____
4. Date called: _____

Suggestions for checking by phone:
1. This is (identify yourself: name, company, department, title).
2. (Applicant's name) has applied to us for employment.
3. Do you remember this person or do you have a record of this person? _____
4. What were the dates of employment with you?
   From _____ To _____
5. What were the duties and responsibilities? _____
6. What were the supervisory or managerial functions? _____
7. How well did the person perform those duties? _____
8. What do you think were the person's strengths? _____
9. What do you think were the person's weaknesses? _____
10. How well did the person get along with:
    a. Superiors? _____
    b. Fellow employees? _____
    c. Subordinates? _____
11. What was the person's record for:
    a. Punctuality _____
    b. Attendance _____

cont'd

Recruiting: Interviews, References, Tests 73

12. How much was the person being paid?
    (wages, salary, bonus) _____

13. What personal problems did the person have?
    (domestic, financial, alcohol, drugs, gambling, criminal)
    _____

14. Why did the person leave? _____

15. Would you rehire this person? _____ Why? _____

16. What other comments do you have? _____

17. Thank you for your help.

TESTS

How do you know that applicants can do what they say they
can do? By testing, you try to find out before you hire someone.
The alternative is to hire the person, then evaluate on-the-job
performance. When you use the second method, you should hire
the person for a probationary period. Before doing any testing
ask yourself, "What am I trying to find out?"

Tests can be classified under these categories:

1. Intelligence: mental ability and intellectual development.
2. Achievement: knowledge and skill in a particular subject.
   a. Office skills: typing, shorthand, business machines, and
      so on.
   b. Trade skills: electrical, mechanical, carpentry, and so on.
   c. Professional skills: engineers, accountants, managers.
3. Aptitude: the ability to acquire new information and skills.
   Achievement tests measure what a person can do; aptitude
   tests measure potential: can this person be trained?
4. Interests: what does this person like and dislike?
5. Personality: emotional stability and personal adjustment to
   life; mental health.
6. Physical health.

The most reliable tests are those that measure accurately and
consistently what you are looking for. For example, the applicant says, "I am a good typist." Refer to your specifications:
what will the applicant have to be able to type? simple letters?
technical terminology? figures and formulae? filling in forms?
Do you want speed or accuracy? or both? Will the typing be
repetitious or will there be a variety of jobs? Will the person

be copying from legible handwriting or an audio tape? Will the person have to compose answers to letters of inquiry? or do you hope to train the person to do this? Will the person have to answer a telephone and talk to customers? and so on.

Let's suppose that you can test the applicant's abilities. Are the test results indicative of the applicant's regular (normal) skills? If the test results meet your standards, you can hire the applicant on probation. The on-the-job performance under a variety of situations will then determine the accuracy of your hiring decision.

How do you test a bookkeeper or an accountant? You can't very well ask the person to spend a day or several days working in your office recording debits and credits and preparing financial statements, so you have to check the person's credentials. What is the person's accounting education? Is the person a CGA or an RIA? What accounting experience does the person have? What references can you check? If you decide that intelligence, personality, and other characteristics should be measured, then you should get professional help: don't try to be an amateur psychologist. And check the legal aspects of what you plan to do: job applicants have sued prospective employers for using intelligence tests which do not apply to the cultural background of the test takers.

It's difficult, finally, for an employer to be objective about tests. If you believe in tests, you will use them. If you don't believe in them, you won't use them—or else you'll use them reluctantly. One employer hung a horseshoe on the office wall. The horseshoe was inscribed with the word "Tests." A friend asked, "You don't believe in that horseshoe, do you?"

"Of course not!"

"Then why do you have it?"

"Because it works whether you believe in it or not."

SELECTION DECISION

No one can tell you how to make a decision that will result in the selection of the ideal applicant. This statement is realistic, not negative.

Think of the decision-making process you go through when buying a typewriter, a production machine, or a delivery truck. You gather as much factual information as possible. But many of the "facts" come from the seller. And the seller usually tells you the good news and not the bad news about the product. Some products come with guarantees, trial periods, maintenance and repair services, exchanges, refunds, and trade-ins. You analyze the costs and benefits of each product, then compare the advantages and disadvantages of competing products.

So which typewriter do you buy? No two typewriters and their suppliers are directly comparable in all things. Maybe you decide to make a rational choice, then make it—or think you've made it. You might buy the machine with the highest sales: why did you buy that machine? "Because it's the best!" you reply. "Just look at the sales it racks up!" Rational or emotional? You'll never know for certain.

Of course, you can't compare people with machines. A person is complex, changeable, unpredictable, emotional. It's hard for two persons—the employer and the applicant—to find out enough about each other so the two can make a mutual decision; whether or not to work together in the same organization. Your decision to buy the typewriter would be complicated if the typewriter could also assess the prospective purchaser. Your decision to buy is difficult enough without this added dimension.

Based on limited information about the job applicant, your decision can be rational, emotional, or a combination of rational and emotional. Based on limited information about the organization and the job functions, the applicant's decision can also be rational, emotional, or a combination of rational and emotional.

If you do all the rational things in recruitment and make an objective decision, you should get the person you are looking for. When your experience proves that you did select the right person, you can give credit to your good judgement about people —with a little help from luck. In any event, the final selection decision should always be made by the person who will be directly responsible for supervising the new employee.

If the situation requires you to confirm your decision in writing to the applicant, see Exhibits 3-4 and 3-5 for examples of letters.

Confirmation of Strategy

After you have hired the applicant, refer to your selection strategy. Did you follow your strategy? If not, why not? Should your strategy be changed?

Exhibit 3-4
Letter to Successful Applicant

ABC Co., Address, City, Postal Code

Date _____

Name _____
Address _____
City _____

Dear _____:
I am pleased to tell you that you have been selected for the position of _____.
Your starting salary will be _____.
Would it be possible for you to begin your employment on _____? If not, please let me know the date that will be more suitable for you.
Also, please confirm if you will accept this job and the conditions that we discussed.
Please phone me if you have any questions.

Sincerely,

Name,
Title

Exhibit 3-5
Letter to Unsuccessful Applicant

ABC Co., Address, City, Postal Code

Name _____   Date _____
Address _____
City _____

Dear _____:
I am sorry to tell you that we have decided not to hire you for the position of _____.
Of course it is disappointing when you come so close to getting what you want. But at least you know that you were one of the final few that we considered for the position.
I feel certain that, if you keep trying, you will soon be successful.

Sincerely

Name
Title

4

YOUNG, OLD, AND HANDICAPPED EMPLOYEES

THE YOUNG EMPLOYEE

Many young people do not have marketable skills. Many of these people have not completed their secondary-school or trade-school education. Also, many graduates of secondary schools, colleges, and universities do not have marketable skills. And many do.

All these young people have two things in common. First, they have a great knowledge of the world around them. They have achieved this knowledge through formal education as well as informal—TV, travel, friends. These young people may be well informed as well as misinformed. Second, young people have a changing value structure toward lifestyles and work.

Young People's Attitudes: Do you believe the stereotypes?

The following points are often made about young people in general, but each person should be judged as an individual:

Each person has different needs, has attained a different level of maturity, and has developed a different outlook on life.

Young people are less submissive to authority. They want to be treated as equals and in a humane way. They want the same rights as their boss.

Young people will not tolerate adverse working conditions. Work should be done in pleasant and comfortable surroundings. They are also concerned about health and safety.

Young people do not want jobs that require a lot of physical work. They have been educated to use their brains and not their muscles. They have been trained and conditioned into using cars instead of feet. Also, if they want something done, they think they just have to push a button. They don't believe that hard work is necessary for success.

Young people do not understand the length of time needed to make a decision or bring about change. A delayed decision is interpreted as management's attempt to avoid the issue. Time, to them, is more of an irritant than a resource.

Young people have very little knowledge about how business operates. They believe in the free-enterprise system, but they take the system for granted. Unless they have had a business education, they don't understand why an organization is in business and how it stays in business. On payday they expect to be paid. It's unthinkable that the money won't be there.

Young people do not want boring jobs.. They want a challenging job. But today's youth has been trained more and more to do less and less. Many lower-level jobs are routine and repetitious. A minimum of training and experience is needed to perform these jobs. Machines are doing what people used to do.

Young people who want advancement and promotion are not willing to wait many years for this to happen. They feel confident they can handle more responsibility although their manager knows they have not had the variety of experience or do not have the business maturity that are prerequisites.

Young people are generally interested in other people. They prefer to work with people and care about people. Many of them have good inter-personal skills. Friendship is important in job satisfaction.

Young people have different social, cultural and personal values toward authority, work, sex, marriage, religion and money. Every person, regardless of age, brings a value system to the workplace. An employer must remember that the whole person has been hired.

A young person wants to be recognized as an individual person. There is a need to express this individuality through freedom, self-expression and self-determination. Young people want to decide things for themselves, even if it means making mistakes. Many admit they don't know what they want but they want an opportunity to try to find out what they think they want.

Young people want instant material success. This is an affluent age. Everything imaginable is available—for a price. There is an abundance of goods and services. A young person may not understand that postponement of a purchase may be necessary. "All I need is more money." And the employer is expected to provide it. Hard work, thrift, and long apprenticeships are not considered to be stepping stones for success.

There are young people who are contradictory to the point just made. These people are less interested in material success. They want a richer life but not in terms of money. They have to feel that the work they do is useful and has meaning. Their work should have a purpose other than to make money. They do not care about the employer's need for more sales, lower costs and higher profits. They want a more intrinsic reward.

Young people are not interested in competing with other people in order to achieve success. The business environment might eventually condition them to be competitive. But in the meantime they are more concerned with their own progress than the performance of others.

Young people are more open and honest. They are not afraid to say what is on their mind. Supervisors are sometimes surprised at this frankness, but at least they know what their young employees are thinking.

Young people have less loyalty to their employer. They do not feel any obligation to stay with one employer longer than they want to. Regardless of the training, experience, good treatment, steady employment, pay increases, or promotions they have received, they will leave if it suits their interests.

Many young people are anti-business. To these people big is bad. They feel that the big organization will dominate them, control them and mold them to be conformists.

In a large organization it is difficult to be an individual. There is no sense of freedom or opportunity for self-expression. An employee has little control over environment or future. The people at the top of the hierarchy are nameless and faceless autocrats, not knowing or caring about the people down below.

Your experience has taught you something about young people. Some of this experience may be contradictory to the sixteen points made above. Here is your opportunity to put in writing how you feel about young people. This space is for you:

_____

_____

_____

_____

_____

_____

_____

Now you know if you are prejudiced for or against young people—or if you can see them as individuals, any one of whom may or may not suit your organization on his or her own strengths and weaknesses.

THE OLDER EMPLOYEE

Because of the high turnover common in young employees or the unavailability of suitable younger applicants, some organizations are recruiting older persons.

No one is getting any younger and everyone is older than someone else. But by tradition and practice an employee becomes an older worker at age 40. Age is a state of mind as well as body. One employer said, "Some of my employees died at 25, but they won't be retiring officially until 65."

Advantages of Hiring Older Workers

Many of the older workers believe in and practice the work ethic. The older worker is more conscientious and works harder.

Turnover is lower. Older persons realize the difficulty in getting employment and are less likely to leave. They are more satisfied with their life and are not looking for a great improvement in their job status.

Their wage and salary needs could be less. Raising a family and paying off the mortgage are big expenses for younger people. A married woman with a grown-up family may seek re-employment. Her reasons for getting a job may not be monetary. Also, the combined husband and wife income more than meets their living expenses.

Older employees are experienced. They need less training and can be productive sooner. Older employees have skills that young people lack and may never have.

Older people accept authoritarian work situations. They understand and respond to the need for rules and discipline. They will conform rather than run the risk of losing their jobs.

An older, experienced supervisor might command more respect than a younger person. The older person also has more experience in dealing with all types of people in a variety of situations.

Lateness is less of a problem. Older people are usually able to get up in the morning. Their lifestyles don't include too many late nights or they save the late nights for the weekend.

Absenteeism is lower. The older employee wants to go to work. Personal matters interfere less with the workday. Their time off is usually for a really good reason, like illness.

Older employees may have fewer accidents because they have learned to practice safety at work. Safety may also result from being less venturesome and less willing to take a chance.

Why Don't Some Employers Want Older Workers?

The interviewer prefers to hire people younger than himself. A young supervisor or manager wants to surround himself with young people rather than oldtimers.

Fringe benefits might be more expensive. There might be increased costs for health and retirement plans.

Health and physical strength may be a problem. Some jobs require strong and healthy people. Absence for illness might be higher.

Their skills are obsolete and retraining might be expensive. Young people seem to be more adaptable to change and can adjust easier. If it is true that people are set in their ways, then old age begins a lot sooner than 40.

Older people are less well educated. They have not kept up to date with the knowledge explosion. Their world is different from the modern business environment.

The generation gap still makes it difficult to mix older and younger employees in the same work groups. There are differences in cultures, experiences, values, and ambitions. They may speak the same language, but they don't communicate effectively.

Older employees might not like working for a young supervisor or manager: they won't like taking orders from someone young. It might be more difficult for a young supervisor to discipline an older person.

Older employees might resist overtime. They don't want the extra money or may be too tired to work a longer day.

YOUNG AND OLD

Here is a quiz you can try on yourself and other supervisors and managers. After you have all answered the quiz independently,

you can compare and discuss the results.
1. If I were starting a business I would recruit
   a. Mostly young people, or
   b. Mostly older people, or
   c. The best qualified regardless of age.
      Give reasons for your answer.
2. A supervisor or manager of a mixed age group should treat older and younger employees differently.
   Do you agree or disagree? Why?
3. I would rather be
   a. a young supervisor of older employees, or
   b. an older supervisor of young employees.
      Which is your choice? Why?

HANDICAPPED PERSONS

Here is another quiz. Rank the persons with these handicaps or disabilities in the order of their acceptability to you. Saying you would react to all persons equally is not an acceptable answer. Use all numbers from 1 to 21: 1 is most acceptable; 21 is least acceptable.

alcoholism	_____	ex-convict	_____
amputee	_____	heart disease	_____
arthritis	_____	hunchback	_____
asthma	_____	mental illness	_____
blindness	_____	mental retardation	_____
cancer	_____	old age	_____
cerebral palsy	_____	paraplegic	_____
deafness	_____	stroke	_____
diabetes	_____	tuberculosis	_____
dwarf	_____	ulcer	_____
epilepsy	_____		

Which handicaps are most acceptable to you? Why? Which are least acceptable to you? Why?

Most people pick the hidden handicaps as being more acceptable. We usually feel uncomfortable among persons who are disabled or disfigured. We also feel uncomfortable about being uncomfortable.

If we contact handicapped persons in situations which emphasize their disabilities, we tend to have negative feelings. But if we contact these same handicapped persons in situations which emphasize their abilities, our attitudes and feelings become more positive. For example, it would be easier to have lunch with an alcoholic in a restaurant which didn't serve alcohol; it would be easier to work beside a dwarf while both of you were seated, rather than walk with the same person to the bus stop; a deaf person would be comfortable operating a noisy machine—and you would feel more comfortable knowing that the deaf person was usefully employed.

Could you employ handicapped people in your business? Would there be any advantages to you? Let's not consider any humanitarian reasons, only business reasons.

First, some handicapped persons have been trained at government centres so that they have skills that will make them employable. These persons have been prepared psychologically as well as physically for most job situations. They want to work. They want an opportunity to prove that they have useful skills. These people don't think of themselves as being handicapped if they can perform satisfactorily. Actually, it is the employer who is handicapped because of negative feelings toward these people.

Second, handicapped employees have lower turnover and absenteeism. Handicapped persons know that they have a difficult time getting a job. When they find suitable employment, they often show their appreciation by becoming loyal employees. Besides, handicapped persons usually have a job that matches their abilities, so they have a more favourable attitude toward their jobs. And a person in a wheelchair who comes to work every day on time sets a good example for all employees.

Another reason is productivity. Handicapped persons are motivated to prove that they are as good or better than people who are not handicapped. For some jobs their handicap is an advantage. The deaf person is not distracted or affected by a noisy environment. A blind person has highly developed senses of hearing and touch. Some studies have shown that when handicapped persons are matched to their jobs, 66% are as productive as "normal" employees, 24% are more productive, and only 10% are less productive. Persons who are not handicapped are sometimes motivated to do better.

A fourth reason is fewer accidents. Handicapped persons usually have fewer accidents than other employees. These employees seem to be more aware of their limitations. They also know that they have to be careful because they don't want to increase their disabilities.

Other Considerations

There are some jobs for which handicapped persons may not be suitable. For example, you don't want to put a handicapped person in a face-to-face public contact job if you think the person's appearance and behaviour will not be acceptable to the public. These same handicapped employees may be excellent for public contact by telephone.

Your other employees may object to working with handicapped people. Persons with hidden handicaps as mentioned, are usually more acceptable than those with visual handicaps. You could give your employees the quiz that you did at the beginning of this section. After completing the quiz, the employees could discuss how they feel about working with handicapped people. You could tell your employees that you plan to hire a handicapped person or persons temporarily or part-time. After the trial period you could assess the handicapped person's suitability and productive effectiveness, then ask your other employees how they feel about continuing to work with handicapped people.

How Should You Supervise Handicapped People?

Treat them the same as everyone else. All employees should be hired on their ability or potential to perform the functions outlined in the job description. All employees' productivity should be evaluated according to the standards of performance for that job. Handicapped persons should not be given special personal treatment any more than you would show favouritism to any other employee. Assess what the person does and not who the person is.

Each person, handicapped or not, is an individual with individual needs. Some of the handicapped person's needs may be more obvious than the needs of other employees. Knowing an employee's needs makes a supervisor's job easier. Employees with disabilities usually know their strengths and weaknesses. They don't want charity or insincere kindness. To be treated as anyone else would probably be a great compliment to a handicapped person. Other employees should be told to behave normally toward a handicapped person. No employee should be expected to be an amateur social worker.

5

DEVELOPING YOUR HUMAN RESOURCES

INDUCTION

Think back to your first day on the job. How did you feel? What questions did you have? This reflection will help you look at induction from the viewpoint of both the employer and the employee.

You have spent a lot of time, effort, and money in recruiting the right person. Think of this new employee as a valuable investment. Treat that investment with tender loving care, especially on the first day—and the following days and weeks too.

What are the things you should consider on Day 1? What should be done? What does the new employee have to do?

Here are some suggestions:

1. Documentation: payroll, income tax, unemployment insurance, pension, health insurance, personal record, union.
2. Hours of work, coffee breaks, lunchtime.
3. Policy on lateness, absenteeism.
4. Policy on authorized time off: illness, holidays, leave of absence.
5. Rules: dress, smoking, parking, telephone.
6. Job duties and responsibilities.
7. Probation.
8. Performance appraisal.
9. Introduction to supervisor, to fellow employees, to work place.
10. Training: on and off the job.
11. Grievances.
12. Safety and health.
13. Overtime.

14. Collective bargaining.
15. Pay, bonuses, incentives.
16. Upgrading, promotion, transfer.
17. Importance of each employee's productivity to the success of the organization.

Ask the employee, "Is there anything we've left out?" "Is there anything we haven't made clear?" Don't ask, "Is there anything you don't understand?": You are asking the employee to reveal ignorance and misunderstanding.

In deciding to work for you, the new employee had to make assumptions about you and the organization. Will these assumptions be confirmed on the first day on the job? First impressions often become fixed impressions. The time and effort you and others make at the beginning will pay off in the new employee's attitude, work habits, and productivity.

Giving a new employee a personal physical place is of particular importance. This place might be a desk, a work bench, or the place where the work will be performed. Try to give each person a sense of belonging and a feeling of importance. These needs are basic to everyone, regardless of job function.

Induction Worksheet

Prepare an induction plan for orientating a new employee (see Exhibit 5-1). At the end of Day 1, have an informal meeting with the new employee. Use the Induction Worksheet as the basis for your discussion. Try to get feedback from the employee about what happened. Show that you care about the employee as a person, not just as a means of production.

The new employee will see friends and/or family after the first day of work. You can be certain your new employee will be discussing you and the new job.

What will happen to your new asset between Days 1 and 2? Will the value increase, decrease, or remain the same? You and your employees will have had a great influence on determining that value.

Exhibit 5-1
Induction Worksheet

Name of new employee _____

What will be done?	Why?	When? Date and Time	Who is responsible?
1.			
2.			
3.			
4.			
5.			
6.			
7.			
8.			

PERSONNEL RECORDS

A good record system will help you be a more effective manager. Some records are necessary for business reasons; some, for legal reasons. Whatever the system you establish, make certain that the system works for you—not the other way around. You should keep these records:

1. A personal file for each employee should contain the resumé, application form, reference checks, documents, correspondence, performance appraisals, income-tax forms, certificates of age for minors.
2. Pay. The record should show:
   a. Gross pay
   b. Legal deductions: income tax, Canada Pension Plan, Unemployment Insurance premiums, government health insurance
   c. Other deductions: company pension, Canada Savings Bonds, union dues, group insurance
   d. Net Pay
      The method of payment can be by cash, cheque, or bank deposit. Some banks and companies that provide accounting services will record and calculate wage and salary payments for small companies.
3. Wage or salary increases.
4. Holidays: entitlement and time used.
5. Attendance and punctuality.
6. Illness.
7. Accidents and injuries.
8. Promotions, transfers, upgrading, job reclassification, demotion.
9. Training and development courses.
10. Grievances.
11. Disciplinary action.

All information must be accurate, up to date, and readily available to authorized persons. Only record and store information that is essential to meet the goals of your organization. Exhibit 5-2 shows some of the legal requirements.

Exhibit 5-2
Record Retention

*The federal and provincial governments have legal require-
ments for the retention of personnel records by companies.
Below are some excerpts from the Ontario Ministry of Labour.
These extracts from legislation are reprinted verbatim without
interpretation.*

Note: *A retention period of "not stated" means that the
legislation is not specific on the retention period. These extracts are used to make the reader aware of some of the legal
requirements for maintaining and retaining records. The information below is not necessarily all-inclusive or up to date.*

EMPLOYMENT STANDARDS ACT
S.O. 112/74   Ministry of Labour

Section 11:
1. An employer shall,
    a. make and keep in Ontario or in a place out of Ontario
       authorized by the Director for a period of twenty-four
       months after work is performed or services are supplied
       by an employee complete and accurate records in re-
       spect of the employee showing,
        i) the employee's name and address,
        ii) the employee's date of birth, if the employee is a
            student under eighteen years of age,
        iii) the number of hours worked by the employee in
            each day and week,
        iv) the employee's wage rate and gross earnings,
        v) the amount of each deduction from the wages of the
            employee and the purpose for which each deduction
            is made,
        vi) any living allowance or other payment to which the
            employee is entitled,
        vii) the net amount of money being paid to the em-
            ployee, and
        viii) any documents or certificates relating to pregnancy
            leave under Part XI; and . . .
    Retention Period: Two years after work performed is com-
    pleted.

    b. make and keep in Ontario or in a place out of Ontario
       authorized by the Director for a period of five years after
       work is performed by an employee complete and accu-
       rate records in respect of the employee showing,

cont'd

   i) the employee's name and address,

   ii) the date of commencement of employment and the anniversary date thereof, and

   iii) the employee's wages during each pay period and vacations with pay or payment under section 31.

2. Subclause iii of clause a. of subsection 1 does not apply in respect of the salaried employees of an employer who perform work of a clerical or administrative nature where the employer makes and keeps a record showing the number of hours worked by such employees in excess of eight hours a day and forty-four hours a week.

  Retention Period: Five years after work is performed.

Section 16:

4. Every employer shall keep a register and enter therein the name and address of every homeworker to whom the employer gives homework, and the wages paid therefor.

  Retention Period: Not stated.

INDUSTRIAL STANDARDS ACT
R.S.O. 221 (1970) Ministry of Labour

Section 13:

1. An employer to whom a schedule applies shall make and keep, or cause to be made and kept, for a period of at least twelve months after work is performed by an employee, a record of the name, address, wage rate, vacations with pay or payment in lieu of vacations, hours worked and actual earnings of the employee and such other information as the regulations may require.

  Retention Period: Twelve months after work performed.

R.R.O. 457 (1970)

Section 2:

  In addition to the information required by section 13 of the Act, an employer shall include in the record, and keep for a period of at least twelve months after work is performed by an employee,

  a. the amount of wages paid to each employee for the work performed by him,

   i) during the regular working day and the regular working week, and

   ii) other than during the regular working day or the regular working week,

  established by any Schedule that applies to the employee and the date of the payment;

cont'd

b. the hourly, daily, weekly or monthly rate used in computing wages paid to an employee on time-work;

c. the amount of each kind of work performed by an employee who is paid on a piece-work or unit-price rate on an incentive or production basis and the piece-work rate or unit-price rate used in computing his wages;

d. the period of any vacation taken by an employee and the amount of vacation pay paid to the employee or the payment in lieu of vacation with pay and the date of the payment in each case;

e. the rate of commission or percentage used in computing the wages of an employee who is paid on a commission or percentage basis;

g. the number of hours of work performed by each employee,
   i) during the regular working day and the regular working week, and
   ii) other than during the regular working day or the regular working week,
   established by the Schedule that applies to the employee;

h. the hours of the day and each day of the week on which work was performed by each employee;

i. the work or operation performed in the industry by an employee and where a schedule classifies employees, the classification of the employee;

j. the city, town, village or township where the work or operation was performed; and

k. the number of hours in each day and week that an employee was required to remain on the employer's premises and was not required to perform any work.

Retention Period: Twelve months after work performed.

WORKMEN'S COMPENSATION ACT
R.O. 6 (1971) Ministry of Labour
Section 5:

Every employer shall keep a record of all circumstances respecting an accident as described by the injured workman, the date and time of its occurrence, the names of witnesses, the nature and exact location of the injuries to the workman and the date, time and nature of each first-aid treatment given.

Retention Period: Not stated.

EMPLOYMENT STANDARDS

The federal and provincial governments have employment standards that apply to employees and employers within their respective jurisdictions.

Information from the Employment Standards Act of Ontario is reprinted on the following pages. This information has been prepared for convenience only. For accurate reference, recourse should be had to the official volumes. This information is presented as a general guide for all readers. Those employers not subject to Ontario laws should refer to the acts of government that apply to them.

CONTENTS

1. GENERAL COVERAGE AND APPLICATION: WHO'S COVERED

The Employment Standards Act *applies* to *employees* and *employers* in the *Province of Ontario.* It *does not* apply to persons employed in industries under the jurisdiction of the federal government, such as post offices, railways, airlines, banks, grain elevators, shipping companies, radio and television stations, or police employed by a municipality. Nor do the parts of the Act relating to hours of work, minimum wage, overtime pay, public holidays and vacation pay apply to:
a. qualified practitioners of: architecture, chiropody, dentistry, law, medicine, optometry, pharmacy, professional engineering, psychology, public accounting, surveying or veterinary science;
b. a registered drugless practitioner;
c. a student training for the professions mentioned above;
d. a teacher as defined in The Teaching Profession Act;
e. a person engaged in commercial fishing;

f. a domestic servant employed directly by the householder;
g. a student working under a work-experience program approved by the Ministry of Education or by a community college or university;
h. a registered real-estate salesperson;
i. Crown employees.
j. a salesperson receiving commissions who sells away from the employer's establishment,
k. a person employed on a farm whose employment is directly related to the primary production of eggs, milk, grain, seeds, fruit, vegetables, maple products, honey, tobacco, pigs, cattle, sheep, and poultry. Special conditions apply to persons employed in the harvesting of fruit, vegetables, and tobacco, as set out in item 13 of this bulletin.

A person employed in landscape gardening, mushroom growing, the growing of flowers, trees, or shrubs for the retail and wholesale trade, the growing, transporting and laying of sod, the boarding and breeding of horses, or the keeping of fur bearing animals as defined in the Fur Farms Act is entitled to minimum wages and vacation pay for all of their work. Overtime pay, public holiday pay, and the limitations of hours of work do not apply to these workers.

2. HOURS OF WORK

An employee shall not work more than eight hours a day or 48 hours a week. The Director may, by permit, approve a regular work day of more than eight hours but not in excess of 12 hours, where the employees and the employer jointly agree on the arrangement.

Any employer wishing employees to work more than eight hours a day or 48 hours in a week must apply to the Director of the Employment Standards Branch for a permit. Such a permit may then be issued at the Director's discretion.

Although an employer has a permit allowing extra hours, an employee cannot be required to work over eight hours in a day, or 48 hours in a week, without the consent of the employee or the employee's agent, except in the case of an emergency.

A permit allowing extra hours does not relieve the employer from the requirement to pay overtime pay as required by the Act and Regulations.

An employee may not work more than five consecutive hours without receiving at least a one-half hour eating period.

These standards on *hours of work* do not apply to those persons exempted in Part 1 of this bulletin, as well as:
a. employees whose only work is supervisory or managerial;
b. a full-time firefighter as defined in The Fire Departments Act;
c. a person employed as a fishing or hunting guide;
d. a person employed in construction;
e. a person performing homework;

f. a superintendent of a residential building who resides in the building;

g. an embalmer or a funeral director;

h. a homemaker.

The Act no longer requires employers to provide private transportation for female employees finishing or starting work between the hours of midnight and 6:00 AM or prohibits females under the age of 18 years from working after midnight.

3. MINIMUM WAGE

General, hourly rate .... $ 3.00

Hourly rate for *persons employed to serve liquor*
in licensed premises 2.50

Learner, hourly rate
(applies only during the first month of employment) 2.55

Construction, hourly rate
(includes guards at construction site. No learner rate
or student rate allowed in construction) 2.90

Student, hourly rate
This rate applies to students under 18 who work 28 hours
per week or less during the school term and where the
student works more than 28 hours per week during
school holidays. There is no learner rate for students 2.15

Ambulance Drivers & Helpers
a. weekly rate 127.20
b. where employee works less than 48 hours a week 2.65

Hunting or Fishing Guides
a. for less than 5 consecutive hours 12.50
b. for 5 or more hours whether or not such hours
are consecutive 25.00

Homemakers The hours of work in respect of which a homemaker is to be paid at least the minimum wage of $2.65 per hour shall be not more than 12 hours in a day.

Room and Board

The following maximum rates apply when room and board are included in calculating the *minimum* wage:
Room, weekly $11.00
Meals (each) 1.15
       (weekly) 24.00
Room and meals, weekly 35.00

Employees required to report for work, who work less than three hours, must be paid for at least three hours at the minimum wage, unless they are hired to work less than three hours a day, or are students.

For the purpose of enabling a handicapped person to be gainfully employed, the Director may, on the application of the handicapped person, or the handicapped person's employer and with the consent of the handicapped person, or the handicapped person's parent or guardian, authorize the employment of such handicapped person to perform such work as is authorized at a wage lower than the minimum wage prescribed under this Act.

Employees exempt from minimum wage are those exempted in Part 1 of this bulletin as well as:

a. a student supervising children;
b. a student employed at a camp for children;
c. a student employed in a recreation program operated by a charitable organization;
d. a superintendent of a residential building who lives in the building;
e. a person training to be a registered nurse or registered nursing assistant;
f. a person training as a laboratory technologist or radiological technician;

Note

1. Liquor in the Liquor Licence Act is defined as "Spirits, wine and beer or any combination thereof and includes any alcohol in a form appropriate for human consumption as a beverage alone or in combination with any other matter."
2. The minimum wage rate of $2.50 applies to a person employed to serve liquor in licensed premises whether or not they actually serve liquor. Premises means that part of the establishment that is licensed and includes a room service situation where the hotel is so licensed, and a place for which a Permit has been issued under the Liquor Licence Act.

    If the work environment is such that a person might serve liquor, the rate applies even though on that particular shift the employee did not actually serve liquor. Shifts or pay periods need not be split. Employees who serve liquor for any part of the pay period will receive the $2.50 rate for the entire pay period.
3. There is no learner rate attached to the $2.50 rate.

4. HOMEWORKERS

No person shall employ a homeworker without a permit issued by the Director of the Employment Standards Branch.

Where a homeworker is paid on piece-work rates, the rates must be high enough to ensure that the employee is able to earn not less than a minimum wage. Homeworkers are entitled to vacation pay.

Hours of work, public holidays, overtime, and learner-rate provisions do not apply to a homeworker. Homeworker does not mean a domestic servant, but rather a person doing work at home which would ordinarily be done in a shop or office.

5. PUBLIC HOLIDAYS

Employees are entitled to seven public holidays *with pay:* New Year's Day, Good Friday, Victoria Day, Dominion Day, Labour Day, Thanksgiving Day, and Christmas Day.

An employee *does not* qualify for a paid holiday if the employee:

a. is employed for less than three months;
b. does not work on twelve days of the four *work weeks* preceding the holiday;
c. does not work on his or her *regular* day of work preceding and following the holiday;
d. having agreed to work on a public holiday, does not report for and perform the work without reasonable cause;
e. is employed under an arrangement where he or she may elect to work or not when requested so to do.

Public holiday benefits apply to full-time, part-time, and student employees.

The regular rates of wages of an employee whose hours of work differ from day to day, or who is paid on a basis other than time, shall be the average of the employee's daily earnings exclusive of overtime for the days worked in the 13-week period immediately preceding a public holiday.

Where a public holiday falls on a working day for an employee, an employer may *with the agreement of the employee or employee's agent,* substitute another working day for the public holiday, which day shall not be later than the next annual vacation of the employee, and the day so substituted shall be deemed to be the public holiday.

If the holiday falls on a non-working day, the employee shall be given another normal working day off with pay, or, if the employee agrees, the employer will pay the employee the regular wage for the public holiday.

Premium Pay for Working on the Public Holiday

If a qualified employee does not have a substitute arrangement and works on a public holiday, the employee must be paid at least time and one-half the regular rate for those hours worked, in addition to the employee's regular day's pay for that public holiday.

Where an employee is employed in a *hotel, motel, tourist resort, restaurant, tavern, continuous operation,* or a *hospital,* and the employee is required to work on a public holiday, the employer may pay the employee regular wages for work done on the public holiday and give the employee a day off with pay on the first working day following the employee's annual vacation or any other agreed working day; or the employer shall pay the employee for each hour worked, a premium of no less than one and one-half the employee's regular rate, in addition to the employee's regular wages for the public holiday.

An employee who *does not qualify* for a paid holiday must be paid at least time and one-half the employee's regular rate for each hour worked on New Year's Day, Good Friday, Victoria Day, Dominion Day, Labour Day, Thanksgiving Day, and Christmas Day.

No *public holiday pay* is required for those persons exempted in Part 1 of this bulletin as well as:
a. a full-time firefighter as defined in The Fire Departments Act;
b. fishing or hunting guides;
c. homeworkers;
d. a student supervising children;
e. a student employed at a camp for children;
f. a student employed in a recreation program operated by a charitable organization;
g. a superintendent of a residential building who lives in the building;
h. a taxi driver;
i. a seasonal employee in a hotel, motel, tourist resort, restaurant, or tavern who is provided with room and board;
j. a person employed in construction and receives 7% or more of the hourly rate or wages for vacation pay or holiday pay.

6. OVERTIME PAY

With certain exceptions, at least time and one-half the regular rate must now be paid after 44 hours in a week.

The *regular rate* is *the wage rate for an hour of work* in a regular non-overtime work week; or if this not specified, then the *regular rate* is the average hourly rate calculated by dividing the wages of an employee earned in a week by the number of hours the employee worked in that week.

The hours an employee has worked on a public holiday, *for which the employee received premium pay,* are not included for the purpose of calculating overtime pay for the same work week (see examples).

There is no provision in the Act for overtime pay on a daily basis.

Overtime benefits apply to full-time, part-time, and student employees.

Special regulations for overtime pay apply to employees working in: sewer and watermain construction industry; road building industry; local cartage industry; seasonal employee in hotel, tourist resort, restaurant, and tavern industry; highway transport industry; seasonal employees in fruit- and vegetable-processing industry; and the ambulance-service industry.

The Director of Employment Standards may approve an arrangement for the averaging of hours of work over a period of two or more weeks for overtime-pay purposes.

Approvals that may be granted must meet the following criteria:

a. a *regular* work schedule is established over the averaging period;
b. the employees or their agent are in agreement with the arrangement.

No *overtime pay* is required for those persons exempted in Part 1 of this bulletin as well as:

a. a full-time firefighter or defined in The Fire Departments Act;
b. an employee whose only work is managerial or supervisory in character;
c. fishing or hunting guides;
d. homeworkers;
e. a student supervising children;
f. a student employed at a camp for children;
g. a student employed in a recreation program operated by a charitable organization;
h. a superintendent of a residential building who lives in the building;
i. a taxi driver;
j. a homemaker.

Computing Overtime, Premium, and Public Holiday Pay

Example 1: Week in which there is no public holiday

Sun.	Mon.	Tues.	Wed.	Thurs.	Fri.	Sat.	
0	8	13	8	8	8	8	= 53 hours

Rate $3.00 per hour

Regular	44 × $3.00 = $132.00
Overtime pay	9 × $4.50 = $ 40.50
Totals	53 hours $172.50

Example 2: Qualified employee in week of public holiday

Sun.	Mon.	Tues.	Wed.	Thurs.	Fri.	Sat.	
0	(0)	13	8	8	8	8	= 45 hours

Rate $3.00 per hour
Monday is a public holiday

Public holiday pay	(8 × $3.00) = $ 24.00
Regular	44 × $3.00 = $132.00
Overtime	1 × $4.50 = $ 4.50
Totals	45 hours $160.50

Example 3: Employee qualified for public-holiday pay

Sun.	Mon.	Tues.	Wed.	Thurs.	Fri.	Sat.
0	(8)	13	8	8	8	8 = 53 hours

Rate $3.00 per hour
Monday is a public holiday

Public holiday pay	(8 × $3.00) = $ 24.00
Premium holiday pay	(8 × $4.50) = $ 36.00
Regular	44 × $3.00 = $132.00
Overtime	1 × $4.50 = $ 4.50
Totals	53 hours $196.50

Example 4: Employee not qualified for public-holiday pay

Sun.	Mon.	Tues.	Wed.	Thurs.	Fri.	Sat.
0	(8)	13	8	8	8	8 = 53 hours

Rate $3.00 per hour
Monday is a public holiday

Premium holiday pay	(8 × $4.50) = $ 36.00
Regular	44 × $3.00 = $132.00
Overtime	1 × $4.50 = $ 4.50
Totals	53 hours $172.50

7. VACATION PAY

After one year of service, employees are entitled to two weeks' vacation with pay. The vacation pay must be at least 4% of the total wages for the year for which the vacation is given.

An employee who terminates before completing one year of service, must receive 4% of total wages calculated from the first day employed.

Total wages include all money received by an employee from the employer, as well as the value of room and board as set out in the Regulations, but does not include:

a. tips and gratuities;
b. any money paid to an employee solely at the discretion of the employer and not based on any performance over which the employee has control;
c. expenses and travel allowances;
d. money paid on behalf of employees to insurance plan;
e. previously paid vacation pay.

The employer shall decide when the vacation is given. It may be a two-week period or two periods of one week each. The two weeks' vacation must be given within ten months after the employee has earned it.

The employee's vacation pay entitlement must be paid within one week of termination of employment.

Vacation pay benefits apply to full-time, part-time, and student employees.

No vacation pay is required for those persons exempted in Part 1 of this bulletin as well as:

a. a person training to be a registered nurse or registered nursing assistant;

b. a person training as a laboratory technologist or radiological technician.

8. EQUAL PAY FOR EQUAL WORK

No employer or person acting on behalf of an employer shall differentiate between male and female employees by paying a female employee at a rate of pay less than the rate of pay paid to a male employee, or vice versa, for *substantially* the same kind of work performed in the same establishment, the performance of which requires *substantially* the same skill, effort, and responsibility, and which is performed under similar working conditions, except where such payment is made pursuant to:

a. a seniority system;

b. a merit system;

c. a system that measures earnings by quantity or quality of production; or

d. a differential based on any factor other than sex.

What Does It Mean to the Employer?

1. *What does equal pay mean?*

   If persons of opposite sexes are performing substantially the same work in the same establishment under similar working conditions, you cannot pay them less because of sex only.

2. *When was the Equal Pay Act put into effect?*

   Initially in 1951 under the "Female Employees Fair Remuneration Act," which was incorporated in 1962 into the "Human Rights Code" and on January 1, 1969, into The Employment Standards Act, which is currently administered by The Employment Standards Branch.

3. *Does this law apply to males as well as females?*

   Yes.

4. *If two persons of the same sex do the same work, and one is paid less than the other, could that employee make a claim for equal pay?*

   No—comparisons may only be made between persons of opposite sex.

5. Does the work have to be exactly the same?

No—where the work is substantially similar an equal pay situation may exist.

6. Can a person of one sex doing the same work as a person of the opposite sex be paid less for any reason?

Yes—provided it is because of a factor other than sex; i.e., a seniority system, a merit system, or a system that measures by quality or quantity of production, i.e. piece work.

7. If a person of the opposite sex replaces an employee as lead hand, and does substantially the same work as the employee replaced performed, but is paid less than the employee replaced, can that person launch a claim under equal pay?

Yes—providing the work done required substantially the same effort, skill, and responsibility; and the former employee was not paid a higher rate because of a seniority system, merit system, or a piece-work system, etc.

8. If work done by one sex is different than the work done by persons of the opposite sex, but is worth as much to the company, could there be a claim?

No—the Act applies only to equal pay for equal work, not to work of equal value.

9. Should a female working as a sales clerk in the ladies' wear department receive the same pay as a man working as a sales clerk in the men's wear department?

Yes—providing the work done is substantially the same as the higher paid person, requiring equal skill, effort, and responsibility.

10. Can a claim under equal pay be made if an employer will not allow a female employee to apply for a higher-paying job performed by a male?

No—however, the Human Rights Code prohibits such discrimination in employment practices on the basis of sex. The employee should contact the local Human Rights Office.

11. Are names revealed to employers if claims are filed?

No—names are not revealed without permission.

12. Can a person be fired because a claim is made for equal pay?

No—an employer cannot fire an employee for this reason.

13. If a claim is successful, could an employer reduce the wages of a higher-rated person of the opposite sex, rather than give the lower-rated person a raise?

No—an employer may not reduce the wages of an employee in order to comply with the Act.

14. *Does Equal Pay for Equal Work apply to all types of business and industry?*

Yes—with the exception of employees under Federal Government Legislation who are protected under The Canada Labour Code.

15. *Do qualifications or experience make the difference when deciding equal pay cases?*

Only when related to the work being done.

16. *If, since being hired, more duties are given to the female employee, so that the work now being done is substantially similar to work being done by male employees who are receiving more money, can an employer continue to pay the female employee at the lower rate at which she was hired?*

No—providing the work done is substantially the same as the higher-paid person requiring equal skill, effort, and responsibility, and is not based on a seniority system, merit system, or a piece-work system.

17. *What is skill?*

Skill is the ability and qualifications to apply oneself to the job. Skill includes consideration of such factors as experience, training, and education.

18. *What is effort?*

Effort is the measurement of the physical or mental exertion needed for the performance of the job.

19. *What is responsibility?*

Responsibility is the degree of accountability required in the performance of the job.

20. *What is an establishment?*

It is a physical place of business rather than an entire enterprise (the enterprise being all branches or locations).

21. *To exclude a person from Equal Pay for Equal Work, must all the exceptions be met (see the Act above)?*

No—any one exception would exclude a person from Equal Pay for Equal Work.

22. *If the job being done by a female requires more skill than the job being done by a male, but the job being done by the male requires much more effort, could there be a claim under Equal Pay?*

No—skill cannot be offset by effort, etc.

23. *Could a person be temporarily assigned to a position working*

with a person of the opposite sex with either a greater or lesser rate of pay?

Yes—in emergency situations of short duration.

24. *Does equal pay apply to part-time employees and students?*

Yes—when compared with employees in similar circumstances.

25. *Does equal pay apply to persons paid on commissions?*

Yes.

26. *A union agreement provides that female waiters be paid 20¢ an hour less than male waiters working in the same place. Should the female waiters be paid the same as the male waiters?*

Yes—if the work is the same. That part of the union contract setting separate rates would be invalid.

27. *Are all investigations based on complaints?*

No—routine inspections are conducted.

28. *How can employees and employers get more information?*

Contact the Employment Standards Branch.

29. *How can a complaint be made?*

By calling in person, phoning, or writing a letter to your nearest Employment Standards Branch.

9. BENEFIT PLANS

No employer can differentiate between employees, classes of employees, or their beneficiaries, because of *age, sex* or *marital* status, concerning a fund or plan offered to employees by an employer as a condition of employment, or a voluntary plan.

This applies to plans which provide for superannuation, retirement, unemployment, income replacement, death, disability, sickness, accident, or medical, hospital, nursing or dental expenses, or other similar benefits. Benefits under a deferred profit-sharing plan, where profits are permitted to be withdrawn or distributed upon death, retirement, or some other contingency are also included.

10. PREGNANCY LEAVE

An employee is entitled to 17 weeks of unpaid leave of absence for pregnancy, where she has been employed with her employer for at least 12 months and 11 weeks.

An employee who qualifies for pregnancy leave cannot be terminated or laid off because of her pregnancy.

An employer must give 17 weeks' leave of absence for pregnancy to an employee who requests and qualifies for pregnancy leave.

This leave may commence at any time during the 11 weeks prior to the estimated date of delivery.

An employee on leave of absence as a result of pregnancy must receive six weeks' leave after the date of actual delivery. A shorter period of time may only be granted with approval by her physician.

An employee must give two weeks' notice in writing, together with a medical certificate estimating date of delivery, to the employer when applying for leave of absence due to pregnancy.

An employee who is entitled to leave and has not applied shall be granted a leave if before the expiry of two weeks after ceasing to work she provides her employer with a medical certificate stating she was not able to work and giving the estimated or actual date of delivery.

An employee, after giving one week's notice to her employer, and on receiving a doctor's certificate, may shorten the postnatal six weeks' leave of absence.

When the employee returns to work, the employer must reinstate her to the same job at the same wages with seniority and benefits accrued as at the date of leaving. If her original is not available, she will be assured of reinstatement to a comparable job.

The employer is not required to pay wages to an employee while she is on pregnancy leave.

This benefit applies to full-time, part-time, and student employees.

11. TERMINATION OF EMPLOYMENT

An employee who has worked *three months or more* must be given written notice of termination by the employer of at least:
1. one week if employee worked less than two years;
2. two weeks if employee worked two years but less than five years;
3. four weeks if employee worked five years but less than ten years;
4. eight weeks if employee worked ten years or more.

Notice of termination applies to full-time, part-time, and student employees.

Only after written notice has been given and the time of notice has expired can the employee be terminated.

If an employer wishes to terminate an employee without notice, the required written notice of termination must still be given and normal wages for a non-overtime week must be paid for the number of weeks the employee is entitled to notice. Full vacation pay entitlement must also be paid to the employee.

Where an employer is terminating 50 or more employees in a period of four consecutive weeks, special conditions will apply.

The employer is not required to give notice to an employee if:
a. the employee was hired for a specified term or task—that is, a pre-arranged period of time, or a specific unit of work that does not exceed 12 months;

b. an employee is only temporarily laid off, not terminated (i.e., a period of 13 weeks or less). In the event the employee is not called back by the employer after 13 weeks, it must be treated as a termination;
c. an employee is guilty of wilful misconduct, disobedience or neglect of duty;
d. the work agreement is impossible of performance or frustrated by a fortuitous or unforeseeable event or circumstance; as in fire or flood, but not insolvency or bankruptcy;
e. an employee is engaged in construction work;
f. an employee is terminated at retirement age, as a result of an established company practice;
g. an employee has refused reasonable alternate work (with the same employer);
h. an employee has refused alternate work available through a "bumping" system;
i. an employee who does not return from layoff within a reasonable time when requested to do so by the employer;
j. an employee who may elect to work or not for a temporary period as an arranged condition of employment with the employer.

12. GENERAL ADMINISTRATION

An employee cannot be dismissed or suspended because of a garnishment issued against the employee's wages.

An employer shall give an employee a wage *statement* showing what the wages are paid for, the rate, the gross wages, the amount of deductions and the net amount paid to the employee.

A *vacation pay statement* must be given the employee by the employer at the time the vacation pay is paid to the employee. This statement will show the time or work vacation pay is paid for, the total pay on which the vacation pay is being calculated, the amount of each deduction and its purpose, and the net amount of vacation pay being paid to the employee.

Records

Every employer shall make and keep in *Ontario* for 24 months after the work is done, *complete records concerning* the employee showing:
1. name and address;
2. date of birth if employee is a student under 18;
3. the hours worked each day and week;
4. rate and gross earnings;
5. the amount and purpose of each deduction;
6. any living allowance or other payment to which the employee is entitled;
7. the net pay;
8. any documents or certificates relating to maternity leave.

Further, an employer shall keep records in *Ontario,* for five years that show the employee's name and address and original date of employment, wages paid for each period, and shall indicate vacations with pay, or any payments made to the employee on account of vacation pay.

The employer is *not* required to record the daily or weekly hours of salaried, clerical, or administrative employees, except where such an employee works over eight hours per day or 44 hours per week.

Business Sale

When a business is sold, if the buyer does not continue the employment of the employee, the responsibility for notice of termination *rests with the seller.*

An employee's time of service cannot be lost through change of ownership or sale of business. The employee's total seniority will count when calculating holiday pay, vacation pay, pregnancy leave, and termination of employment.

Other Provisions

Two or more businesses under common control can be deemed to be one when determining the rights of an employee under this Act.

For the purposes of this Act, where the hourly rate of an employee is not readily determined, provisions within the Act allow the Employment Standards Branch to establish a basis for calculating the regular rate and overtime premiums. A week is defined as seven consecutive days.

Any provision of an employment agreement that gives to an employee a greater benefit than the minimum standards that apply in The Employment Standards Act will be the standard that applies to that employee.

Employment Standards Officers can assist employees to collect wages due up to an amount of $4000 for each employee. A penalty of 10% may be imposed on each collection.

An officer, director, or agent of a corporation, who authorizes, permits, or acquiesces in contravention of the Act can be made a party to a claim for monies due its employees under the Act.

Section 59 of The Employment Standards Act provides that any person found in violation of the Act may, on conviction, be fined up to $10,000 or imprisoned for up to six months, or both.

If the *employer* disagrees with an order of the Director regarding the application of this Act, that decision may be appealed and reviewed by a referee appointed by the Minister of Labour.

An *employee* may appeal to the Director, if an employment-standards officer refuses to issue an order against an employer on behalf of that employee.

The Director may require employers to post notices relating to this Act where they can be seen by employees.

No *deductions* can be made from an employee's wages except required by law, or those agreed to by the employee in *writing.* An employee's written agreement for deductions from wages is *invalid* if it is for damages claimed by the employer or for cash shortages where any other person has access to the cash.

No employee can waive his or her rights as provided by The Employment Standards Act (e.g. premium pay for overtime).

13. AGRICULTURAL WORKERS

Except for persons engaged in the harvesting of fruit, vegetables, or tobacco, a person employed on a farm to produce eggs, milk, grain, seeds, fruit and vegetables, maple products, honey, tobacco, pigs, cattle, sheep, or poultry, is exempt from the parts of the Act dealing with minimum wage, overtime pay, vacation pay, public holiday pay, and hours of work.

Persons employed in the harvesting of fruit, vegetables or tobacco, must receive at least the minimum wage. The employee can be paid on a piecework basis as long as the piecework rate is set at such a level that the average worker under average crop conditions can earn at least the minimum wage.

These same employees, employed for more than three months, will be entitled to vacation pay of 4 per cent of their total wages.

These workers, when employed for more than three months, will be entitled to public holidays with pay, on New Year's Day, Good Friday, Victoria Day, Dominion Day, Labour Day, Thanksgiving Day, and Christmas Day.

The Regulations require the employer to maintain wage records including the name and address of the worker, the hours worked each week, their wage rates and actual earnings of each employee.

The following schedule sets out the minimum wages and the maximum amounts at which meals or room or both, or a house, may be valued for the purpose of determining if the minimum wage has been paid to the employee:

General, hourly rate	$ 3.00
Student, hourly rate	2.15
(this rate applies to students under 18 who work 28 hours per week or less during the school term or work full time during school holidays)	

Room and board

Room, weekly	$11.00
Meals (each)	1.15
(weekly)	24.00
Room and meals, weekly	35.00
House provided with heat, light, and water, weekly	40.00
House, weekly	30.00

Source: Ontario Ministry of Labour.

TRAINING AND DEVELOPMENT

Training and development may be necessary for your new employees and even for your present employees.

New employees might be unskilled and must therefore be trained before they can become productive. They might be skilled, but need familiarization with your organization's techniques or methods of operation. They might be skilled, but have to be retrained because their skills are not directly applicable. "We used to do it a different way where I worked" is a common statement answered by "Learn to do things our way" or "Forget what you learned in school. That's not the way things are done."

Present employees might have to be upgraded to prevent obsolescence when job requirements change. They might be transferred or promoted, so they must learn new skills. They might be needed for new jobs when the organization expands; in this case, the employer has to answer the question, "Is it better to hire someone who has the skills for the new job or to retrain one of my present employees?"

Present employees might also have to learn skills of more than one job because the organization has a variety of outputs which require a flexible staff who can switch from one job to another; or because the survivors of layoffs have to learn the jobs of those who are laid off; or because absentees must be replaced for the duration of their absences.

Some training is done for humanitarian reasons. An employee may be virtually out of a job because of changes in job specifications. The organization may decide to retrain rather than replace the employee with someone who is already trained.

Training also makes good business sense because an employee who has demonstrated good work habits—productivity, attendance, punctuality, interpersonal skills—is worth retraining. The alternative is to hire a trained person who has unknown work habits. Many employers say that a good person is hard to find, so you should try to keep that "good person."

Also, better-trained employees can become more productive employees. No one functions at 100% of capacity, so most of a person's potential is rarely used. However, training can change potential into skill and increased productivity could be the result. Employees who become more productive can help to reduce costs and increase income and profits. You can then pay the more productive employees more money. Increased income might reduce a person's dissatisfaction with present income; a reduction of turnover results.

As employees develop, they become more self-confident and self-reliant. You can give them more responsibility and authority; these employees usually need less supervision. Managers can then spend more time on their own jobs and less on looking after the work of others. Training employees for more responsibility and authority is particularly important for service organizations. Productivity is difficult to measure in these organizations, so more supervisors are needed to monitor the productivity of people.

Responsibility for Training

A small organization has one big advantage over a large organization: the owner or manager is responsible for training employees. As a result, a large organization will probably have its own training manager and training staff. It's true that this training department will have more resources and facilities than a small organization, but this department has one major problem: who is responsible for training? Most large organizations have not satisfactorily answered this question—and many of those that have answered the question correctly have not implemented what they know they should be doing.

The few large organizations that have the most effective training and development programs have made line managers and supervisors responsible for training. The training manager and the training department supply specific expertise to help meet the needs of the line (or hierarchical) organization. This idea has been borrowed from military organizations.

(Many bad things are said about military organizations, but here is one idea that can benefit the owner/manager of a small business. A military battalion might have a supply officer, a transport officer, a medical officer, a signals officer, a weapons officer, and so on. But it doesn't have a training officer. Each battalion has a commanding officer (CO) who is directly responsible for training. The CO can delegate responsibility for supply, transport, health, signals, and weapons, but cannot delegate responsibility for training: the CO is held directly accountable for training. The CO's title should be Commanding and Training Officer.)

In business, management's attitude determines whether or not training will be effective. If large organizations adopted the military idea, then the Chief Executive Officer (CEO) would be designated President and Training Officer.

Why is training so important that it should be the direct responsibility of the CEO? The executives of organizations (large and small) think that they are in business to produce a product or service. True enough, but is their product or service the primary reason or the end result? Many organizations have been successful by deciding that their product or service was the main reason why they are in business. And our high standard of living has resulted from this emphasis on organizational priorities.

But the world of work has changed. More and more organizations are finding that, if they recruit suitable employees, then train and develop them to meet the needs of the employee as well as the organization, they will produce the desired product or service. Management is now trying to determine the needs of employees.

The old and still prevalent attitude is that employees are a means to an end: they are tools of production. The ideal situation results from organizations and employees who have the same needs. The organization is then responsible to help employees meet their personal needs. (See the section, "Understanding Employees," later in this chapter.) This development of employees will produce better long-term results. The priority is on developing people. These trained people then provide the output, whether product or service. This change in priorities doesn't mean that you give the organization away to the employees. Your planning, organizing, and control can still be management functions.

Whether or not you accept this concept of training, you can still have an advantage over a large organization. The owner or manager of a small organization cannot afford a training manager or a training department. Consider this a blessing because the owner or manager will have to be responsible for training and development. As you grow, you can delegate responsibility for sales, accounting, production, service, or whatever. But never delegate directly the responsibility for training.

Methods of Training

On-the-job training (OJT) is the most common form of training in small organizations. The employee learns while performing or attempting to perform the job functions. OJT permits the employee to be productive while learning; therefore, the employer reaps an immediate return on investment in human assets. OJT can be conducted by a manager, a supervisor, or an employee. OJT is the fastest way for a new employee to learn your methods of doing the job. Both the trainer and the trainee receive day-to-day feedback on how well the employee is progressing. This type of training can be geared to the needs and speed of the trainee. It is a form of tutoring whereby the tutor can give the trainee whatever direction, help, and coaching is needed. The wise trainer will also give the employee as much freedom and independence as the newcomer can handle. Effective training should provide confidence as well as competence so that the ultimate aim of self-direction and self-control will be reached. OJT is the ultimate in getting the manager or supervisor directly involved in training subordinates. These same management people should also provide continuing development of all their employees and not just the newcomers.

Apprenticeship training is a form of trade training and is usually administered by a government or a union. The problem is to attract a young person who is willing to undergo several years of training before achieving a qualification or a licence as a trades person.

Canada Manpower Training on-the-Job Program is designed to provide employers with a reimbursement of up to 50% of a trainee's wages during the first half of the training period; 25% during the second half. The program encourages and assists employers in training workers for fields in which skilled help are in short supply. Maximum wage paid by the Department is $118; training periods range from six to 52 weeks. On-the-job training is a more effective means of producing skilled workers than classroom training is. The plan assists industries in solving their own difficulties in acquiring skilled labour for specific fields. The plan also helps the manager meet the high costs of training. Canada Manpower, by the way, has now joined with Unemployment Insurance; together, they've been renamed the Canada Employment and Immigration Commission.

In *off-the-job training,* employees are trained by schools or institutions (including correspondence courses). This training can be for skills to be used in office or factory. (Most management training is done off the job. Employees are usually reimbursed for all or a portion of tuition fees, books, and materials. Some employers pay the employee on successful completion of the training program. Most of the training is done after working hours, but the employee is not paid extra wages or salary.

If an organization has enough employees for a training course, a trainer can be hired to do in-plant and in-office training. For example, the closing time at the end of the workday might be 5 PM. The training course could be scheduled from 4 to 6 PM. The employer pays one hour of wages or salaries and the employees contribute the other hour free.

What Training Can Do

Think of training as an investment in improving human assets. Some training has an immediate payoff, while other training has long-term benefits. But all training should have a primary goal: to help the employee achieve the standards of performance for the job classification.

To justify training, you have to assess it in these terms: what is the effect of training on quantity, quality, cost, and time? Can you see positive changes in behaviour and performance? Does the employee have a positive attitude toward the job? Does the employee have more commitment and willingness to accept more responsibility? Does the employee think that he or she is growing and making progress? Does the employee have a sense of achievement and accomplishment? What has been the effect of the training on the employee's interpersonal relations?

What Training Can't Do

Training is not a cure-all for solving your employees' problems —especially off-the-job training, which may not be tailored to your organization's specific needs. Also, training is not a substitute for insufficient pay and benefits, nor will training overcome a poorly organized work place, inadequate facilities, or ineffective leadership.

The Biggest Problem

After most off-the-job training, if the training is successful, the individual will have learned new skills and behaviours, but the on-the-job environment may not permit these changes to take place. If the employee changes without a corresponding change in the environment, you will have done more harm than good by sending the employee on the training course in the first place.

Co-ordinating Training Needs with Your Organization's Needs

Human resources training should be related to your planning programs and policies. That is, how many persons at various levels, departments, and locations will be needed? when? Job descriptions and Standards of Performance should also be related. Training should be aimed at satisfying the specifics of the job: responsibilities, authority, objectives.

Your human-resources inventory should be taken into account as well. What skills and potentials do your employees have? Performance appraisal is an important consideration as well: how effective are the human resources? The final question you have to answer before deciding to train employees involves recruitment: can suitable human resources be hired?

"We have a training problem" is a frequent complaint made by managers and supervisors. This complaint is based on the gap between what the employee is doing and what the employee should be doing. When you find this gap, ask yourself this question: if the employee's life depended on it, could the employee do the job and meet the performance standards? If the answer is "yes," you don't have a training problem. The problem is motivation.

UNDERSTANDING EMPLOYEES

No single motive determines how all individuals will react in all situations. No single supervisory or management strategy will result in high morale and productivity for everyone all the time.

In trying to understand people, you must first recognize that everyone is an individual and that every individual is complex. Because everyone is an individual, there is no such thing as an average person. Everyone is different from everyone else and each person is a complicated pattern of thoughts, feelings, and actions.

Social scientists have been studying people for years: their job will never end, nor should it. In the meantime, you can benefit from their research and apply it to your job situation. One of the best known and most widely used theories of motivation is Maslow's Hierarchy of Needs. Here is what Maslow discovered:
1. A person is a wanting animal.

2. A person continually strives to satisfy needs.
3. These needs are arranged in a hierarchy of importance.
4. As soon as one of the needs is satisfied, another appears in its place.
5. This is a never-ending process all through life.
6. The needs of the lower level, if unsatisfied, take priority over those at higher levels.
7. A satisfied need does not motivate behaviour.
8. More than one need can be satisfied at the same time, but item No. 6 above always applies.

These individual needs can also become group needs.

See Exhibit 5-3.

The following elaborates on Maslow's Hierarchy:
1. **Physiological needs** These are our basic needs. We need air, water, food, rest, and sleep in order to survive. Bodily functions such as sex and elimination of bodily wastes are physiological needs. For most of us, money is also a basic need for survival. A person's basic needs do not have to be fully satisfied. But how long could you survive if you were deprived of any one need on your list?
2. **Safety needs** We want to feel safe from danger, pain, and accidents. On the job we may feel threatened by arbitrary management actions or an authoritarian boss—or a boss who practices discrimination and favouritism. We feel threatened by layoff, dismissal, or an employer who goes bankrupt.
   We protect ourselves with savings accounts, union contracts, seniority, unemployment and health insurance, pensions, and police and fire services. Unless independently wealthy, every employee from bottom to top in an organization is dependent on someone else for security.
3. **Social needs** We want to live, work, and play with other people. Even when we want to be alone we like to know that other people are around somewhere. Our social needs include belonging, association, acceptance, friendship and love. (Some people are unable to establish relationships with some other person and suffer from loneliness.)
   Many people go to work to satisfy their social needs. Every organization is made up of informal (social) as well as formal (business) groups. Sometimes management misinterprets the purposes of informal groups. Some managers consider these informal groups as a threat to the formal organization. When threatened, members of informal groups could resist, becom-

Exhibit 5-3
Hierarchy of Needs

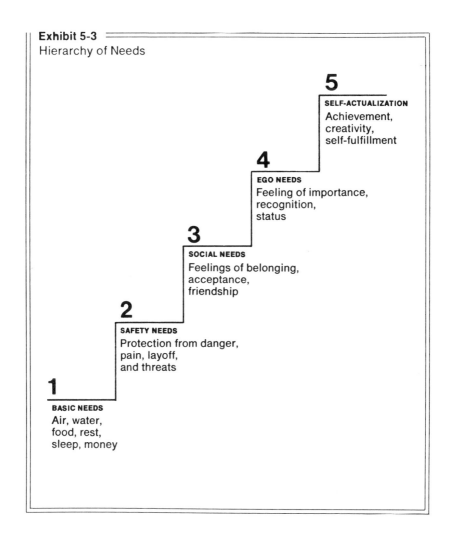

5

SELF-ACTUALIZATION
Achievement,
creativity,
self-fulfillment

4

EGO NEEDS
Feeling of importance,
recognition,
status

3

SOCIAL NEEDS
Feelings of belonging,
acceptance,
friendship

2

SAFETY NEEDS
Protection from danger,
pain, layoff,
and threats

1

BASIC NEEDS
Air, water,
food, rest,
sleep, money

ing antagonistic and uncooperative. This anti-organizational behaviour is usually the result of the manager's attitude and behaviour; the manager assumes that the informal group caused the behaviour.

4. **Ego needs** Everyone wants to feel important. We can satisfy this need through doing something that gives us self-esteem. It can also come from others who recognize our achievements and tell us how good we are: praise and status help to satisfy our egos; we want recognition for our efforts.

On the job we can receive private and public recognition from our fellow employees, our supervisor, and management, whether compliments, indications of respect, or promotions and titles.

Many employees don't receive recognition on the job. Off the job they join social, political, or union organizations where they do receive recognition.

5. **Self-actualization** We try to find self-fulfillment by doing what we like to do: we want to be creative, whether on the job or after work. Some satisfy the need for self-expression through art, music, gardening, or helping other people in some way, for example.

How many people really like what they do and feel that what they do is worthwhile?

LARGE vs. SMALL ORGANIZATIONS

In the job market you are competing with every employer. First, let's look generally at the advantages and disadvantages to the employee in working for large and small organizations. Later we will look at the specific advantages and disadvantages of working for your organization.

Advantages of Working for a Large Organization

1. Prestige and reputation. The well-known organization not only attracts a job seeker, but also provides status and a feeling of importance.
2. Security. The mortality rate is low among large organizations.
3. Training. In addition to on-the-job training there could be formal training programs. The formal training could be in-plant (or in-office) as well as at an off-the-job location such as a community college.
4. Equipment. The large organization can afford and is willing to invest in new equipment for office and factory.
5. Methods. Professional managers are willing to try new methods and techniques. Behavioural scientists, for example, have found fertile ground for employment in large organizations.
6. Fringe Benefits. Large organizations have a long list of fringe benefits—and the benefits get better every year. Applicants expect that all organizations will have these benefits.
7. Advancement. There are many opportunities for being trans-

ferred or promoted. Employees can job hunt inside their own organization.
8. Social. People are social beings and like to associate on the job with other people. Large organizations provide many advantages to applicants who want a job that provides opportunities for establishing interpersonal relationships.
9. Write down other advantages you think of:_____

_____

Disadvantages of Working for a Large Organization

1. Being a specialist. Jobs are fragmented because of the volume of work. The employee becomes a specialist in one job function. The employee could become bored or trapped by this specialization.
2. Policies and rules. Large organizations have policy manuals. There is a written rule for everything. These rules can be inhibiting and threatening. Red tape is real; change can be slow.
3. Formal environment. Large organizations can be very formal in interpersonal and interdepartmental relationships. The employee often translates this formality as being unfriendly.
4. The hierarchy. The employee, psychologically at least, is a long way from the president. The vast organizational structure seems like a jungle.
5. Less easily noticed. "Who am I?" is often answered, "A nobody." The employee's good work may not be noticed or else is taken for granted.
6. Competition. There may be more opportunities for advancement, but many employees may want the same promotion. There is also competition for cultivating the favour of those management persons who decide the fate of employees.
7. Money. Because they attract many applicants, some huge well-known organizations offer lower salaries. Also, internal promotions don't provide the same salary increases as those same employees could get if they changed companies.
8. Seniority. Many organizations say that promotion will be based on merit. Promotion often goes to the senior employee who is considered to be loyal to the organization's policies and procedures.
9. Write down other disadvantages you think of:_____

Advantages of Working for a Small Organization

1. Being a generalist. In a small organization an employee can get a variety of experiences which provide well-rounded training. The employee has opportunities for using more skills and potential. This growth can lead to self-fulfillment and satisfaction.
2. Policies and rules. The lack of written methods of procedures leads to more freedom and flexibility. Rules are often situational, something like the development of common law in our judicial system. Under situational conditions, rules are developed because there is a need and a reason.
3. Informal environment. Many employees say that small organizations are friendlier than large organizations. Interpersonal and interdepartmental relationships are established in a personal rather than in a formal way.
4. Close to the top. Physically and psychologically, each employee is close to top management, so the employee can identify more with the aims of management.
5. Easily noticed. Managers know more about what employees are doing. An employee has an opportunity to become a "somebody."
6. Money. For competitive reasons, small organizations often pay as much or more than large organizations pay to qualified persons.
7. Experience. Untrained and inexperienced persons are sometimes forced to seek employment with small organizations because large organizations may prefer trained applicants. These untrained applicants are willing to accept a lower wage or salary in order to get experience and training.
8. Write down other advantages you think of:_____

_____

_____

Disadvantages of Working for a Small Organization

1. Status. Working for a small and unknown organization is a detriment to the employee who wants to impress others with the reflected image of the prestige and reputation of a large well-known organization.
2. Insecurity. The mortality rate is higher among small organizations.

3. Training. Many applicants have been conditioned to expect formal training programs, but formal training is rare in small organizations.
4. Equipment. The small company may not be able to afford or is unwilling to invest in new equipment. Graduates of schools and training programs expect that every organization will have modern equipment.
5. Methods. Some small-business managers lack formal education and training. These managers learn from their own experience and are not aware or are unwilling to acknowledge that better methods are available.
6. Fringe benefits. The large organizations pioneer in fringe benefits. The small organizations usually lag behind and consider some benefits to be unnecessary expenses.
7. Advancement. Many applicants think that they can join a small organization and grow along with it. These expectations usually turn into disillusionment and disappointment. A growing organization often needs specialized skills to meet new tasks associated with growth. The loyal, hard-working employee who expects to be promoted may lack the education and training that the new job requires; the small organization is then forced to hire someone from outside.
8. Social. New employees sometimes find that working for a small organization is like moving to a small town. The opportunities to socialize are minimal.
It may be true that small organizations are friendlier, but interpersonal relations are more personal and therefore take longer to establish. In a small work group, age, sex, education, and cultural background become more important: Employee compatability could be critical to job success.
9. Flexible. An applicant has to be willing and able to do a variety of tasks, often under the pressure of events over which the employee-to-be will have little or no control. Many employees complain of the faster pace in small organizations.
10. Overtime. A growing organization is chronically understaffed. A small organization also lacks the human resources to cope with fluctuations in the workload. It is easier for an employee in a large department in a large organization to leave unfinished work at the end of the day.
11. Write down other disadvantages you think of:_____
_____
_____
_____

Advantages and Disadvantages
of Working for Your Organization

Here is an opportunity for you to be specific about the advantages and disadvantages to an employee who works for your organization. You have to be objective and look at your organization from the viewpoint of an employee or a job applicant. A check list will help. Here are some suggestions. You should add items of your own.

Item	Advantages	Disadvantages
1. Prestige of job or organization		
2. Reputation of organization's product or service		
3. Job security		
4. Formal training		
5. Office equipment		
6. Factory equipment		
7. Management and supervisory methods and techniques		
8. Fringe benefits		
9. Opportunities for upgrading		
10. Opportunities for transfer		
11. Opportunities for promotion		
12. Opportunities for experience: a. specialist b. generalist		
13. On-the-job social opportunities		
14. Policies and rules		
15. Working conditions: a. physical b. psychological		
16. Wages and salaries		
17. Organizational structure		
18. Communications (between management and employees)		
19. Location		
20. Overtime		
21. Future (organization's growth)		
22. Collective bargaining (union)		

Before looking for job applicants, you should ask your employees what the advantages and disadvantages are of working for your organization. You could ask an employee, "If you were going to recommend this organization as a place of employment for a friend of yours, what would you say to your friend?"

Also, ask your suppliers and customers what they think of you. Make your list complete. Include everything that you think is important and unimportant. It might be unimportant to you, but important to a job applicant and an employee. Your list can also be a method of organizational analysis and organizational improvement.

A. Of the items on my list, which are the items over which I have a. control? b. no control?
B. Of the items over which I have control, which are the ones that I want to a. change? b. leave as is?
C. Of the items I want to change, which are the ones which I will change a. now? b. in the short term? c. in the long term?

HIERARCHY OF NEEDS FOR YOUR ORGANIZATION

You can use Maslow's ideas and apply them to your organization. Refer to your list of the advantages to an employee in working for your organization. Put each item under one of the five categories of needs. Some items might belong to more than one. For example, On-the-job experience provides money (No. 1) and qualifications which give job security (No. 2). An efficient typewriter provides the means for a typist to earn a salary (No. 1) as well as prestige (No. 4). Your location might be convenient for the employee to get to work (No. 2) and to socialize after work or at lunchtime (No. 3).

Training is one of the best examples of satisfying the needs of employees. Training should result in higher qualifications and better skills, which should produce a raise in pay (No. 1). A trained employee will have more job security (No. 2). There are social benefits through interpersonal contact with other persons on the same training course (No. 3).

Being selected by the organization for a training course is a sign of recognition of the importance of the employee (No. 4). If the program permits the employee to use talents for satisfaction and development, the employee will achieve self-actualization (No. 5).

Do your categorizing now:

1. _____

_____

2. _____

_____

3. _____

_____

4. _____

_____

5. _____

_____

You can use this list of the hierarchy of needs for recruiting and on-the-job motivation.

6

MOTIVATION AND MONEY

WAGES AND SALARIES

The importance of money as a motivator is debatable. But one thing is certain—all employees talk about it. Very few employees say they are paid enough—and fewer say they are overpaid. You have to consider four factors when deciding how much to pay your employees.

How much can you afford to pay? For example, the wages of the employees of a highly automated manufacturer might account for 10% of the cost of the product. A 10% wage increase would only add 1% to the manufacturing cost. In a service business, however, wages might account for 80% of the organization's costs. A 10% wage increase would increase costs by 8%.

The manufacturer could increase production by adding a second shift. The machinery and equipment used by the first shift could also be used by the second shift. Maintenance and depreciation costs would increase, but labour costs would still be a small percentage of total costs. If the service organization adds more employees, wage costs will increase substantially. An organization's ability to pay will also be determined by its ability to generate income (sales, collecting receivables, increasing prices) and to reduce costs.

How much is the job worth? Job specifications will help determine the qualifications of the person who will be performing the job. Usually, the higher the qualifications, the higher the pay. Some organizations have a policy: pay the job, not the person. Government regulations will also influence pay rates. There are minimum rates which must be paid. To avoid discrimination, equal pay must be paid for work of equal value. Unions also determine what a job is "worth."

What is the relationship of one person's pay to another person's

within the same organization? Employees will compare their pays to the relative status of their own and other jobs. They will rank the status of jobs as being equal to theirs, higher than theirs, or lower than theirs.

Should a truck driver be paid more than an accountant? Should the person who sweeps the floor be paid more than the person who litters the floor? Should factory (blue collar) employees be paid as much as office (white collar) employees? Employees are sensitive about their relative levels of income. And employers are only fooling themselves if they think pay rates are kept confidential.

An employer can create job status through titles, offices, floor space, desks, rugs, equipment, physical surroundings, washrooms, rest facilities, separate entrances, name plates, reserved parking, dress regulations, special privileges, personal attention, and recognition; the list can go on and on. Some employers deliberately create status. Others do it accidentally or unknowingly.

Employees themselves create status by performing jobs that are difficult (not everyone can do it), dangerous (not everyone is brave), and dirty (not everyone wants to do it). Employees create dress regulations for certain job categories. These dress differences are as distinctive as a uniform. Persons performing certain job categories eat by themselves. And so on.

The wise employer recognizes the relative status of the jobs in the organization. How much the employer pays is an acknowledgement of this status.

Sometimes lower-status jobs receive high pay because of the difficulty of recruiting anyone to do the job. Employees at higher-status jobs will not be happy, but will compensate by demonstrating their status through non-monetary ways. Status will also be affected by subcontracting jobs such as maintenance, repairs, and cleaning. A retail clerk may accept the minimum wage, but might want more money if told to wash the store's windows. A machinist will perform a dirty job as long as someone from the cleaning contractor cleans up the mess left afterwards.

Is an employee who increases productivity rewarded with more pay? Or does everyone receive the same pay increase regardless of performance? An incentive system must be either based on work that is measurable or directly attributable to an employee's (or work group's) efficiency in one or more of these areas: increasing quantity, increasing quality, reducing costs, reducing the time needed. An incentive system must be fair to all employees; the measure must be impersonal and objective. Even so, personal consideration and subjective evaluation are often the basis for monetary rewards.

Incentive pay can come in the form of a piece rate, a bonus, a sharing of cost savings, profit sharing, or a raise in pay. The productivity of some employees is more difficult to measure: all the more reason for a performance-appraisal system which should indicate what is measurable and what is not.

In determining wages and salaries, then, four factors are internal considerations of the organization: the ability to pay, the job specifications, relative status of jobs, and performance of employees.

Three other factors are external to the organization: what competitors pay, what the supply and demand for employees are, and what the cost of living is.

What do your competitors pay? First, who are your competitors? Competitors can be organizations that produce similar products or services, organizations in the same geographic location, organizations that employ similar skills (accountants, typists, drivers, and so on). Other forms of competition are unemployment insurance and welfare payments.

And perhaps the biggest competition of all is government. About 40% of our national income goes to the various levels of local, provincial, and federal governments. Today, governments are often leaders rather than followers in setting pay rates.

What is the supply and demand for employees? In theory, if there are more applicants than jobs, then pay rates should go down; if there are more jobs than applicants, then pay rates should go up.

In practice, several factors can alter this rule of economics. First, we live in an affluent society where some persons prefer unemployment to undesirable work, no matter how high the pay. Second, when jobs are hard to find, many persons return to school, do volunteer work, travel, or do something else that produces satisfaction but little or no income. Third, unemployed persons do not starve to death; governments provide unemployment insurance, welfare payments, housing, health services, and a number of other taxpayer-supported social services; private agencies also perform social services. Finally, unionized employees rarely accept pay cuts: employment may drop, but pay rates remain as high as ever.

Many employees experience the frustration of having a job that no one wants. Even high pay will not attract enough people.

This situation tells the employer something about today's work force: people won't necessarily take a job because they're unemployed or because the money is good.

It also tells applicants something about the types of jobs available. This "job vacancy but no applicants" situation is educating the employer about the motivation of people and educating applicants about the nature of work.

What is the cost of living? It has been going up for so long that the question is not "Will it keep going up?" but "How much has it gone up?" and "What will it be next year?"

When the cost of living goes up or is expected to go up, employees automatically assume that the employer will pay higher wages and salaries. Employers therefore have to keep pace with inflationary costs by raising the prices of their products and services. But if prices go too high, sales may drop. However, if pay rates don't go up, employees will become dissatisfied.

Procedure for Setting Wages and Salaries

Every organization has a pay policy, whether formal or informal, written or unwritten. One of the advantages of a written policy is that you have to think about what you're writing, especially if what you write will be shown to your employees.

Your policy should be based on these five factors:
1. Job specifications: What are the qualifications for each job?
2. Performance appraisal: How well is each employee performing?
3. Relationship of jobs: What is the relative value of each job?
4. Competition: What are other organizations paying for similar jobs?
5. Ability to pay: How will internal and external factors influence the financial welfare (stability) of the organization?

BE YOUR OWN BOSS

One appliance retailer has 15 employees. This retailer gives the employees considerable freedom: they set their own salaries, hours, time off, holidays, and vacations. Employees can also borrow the store's trucks.

When the system was introduced, the employees didn't believe what the boss was saying to them. It took about a month before the employees began to believe in and co-operate with the new style of management. Five years later, the appliance store is still in business. The boss even encouraged the employees to join a retail union, but the union wouldn't compete with the employer in getting wage increases and benefits for the employees.

Should Employees Decide on Their Own Pay?

The subject of pay is a major topic of discussion by employees—and many employees are unhappy with their pay. Or maybe the unhappy employees do most of the talking.

Decisions about wages and salaries are usually made in private by someone at a higher level in the organization. Both managers and subordinates assume that this is the way pay decisions have to be made: it seems logical that the person doing the paying should decide how much each employee should be paid.

Management has other assumptions which may or may not be correct. One of them is that employees don't have the facts or understanding needed to make pay decisions. Another is that, if employees were allowed to make pay decisions, they would think selfishly of themselves and not of the organization's interests and goals.

Fringe benefits are also usually decided by management because management "knows" what is best for employees. Besides, it's more economical if all employees have the same fringe benefits. The result is that many employees are entitled to benefits they neither want or need.

Organizations that have permitted employees to choose their own fringe benefits have found that as many as 80% of employees change their benefits. Most of these employees made responsible decisions that suited the needs of their personal or family situations. Some employees even accepted lower take-home pay in order to increase their benefits.

Pay Raises

Management usually decides when pay raises will be given; an annual pay increase is customary. A salary increase is divided by the number of pay periods, usually 26. After deductions for taxes, pensions, and other fringe costs, very little extra take-home pay is left each payday.

A few organizations have permitted employees to decide how and when the annual increase will be distributed. The options include spreading the increase throughout the year (the 26 method), quarterly installments, semi-annual installments, and a large sum payable at the beginning of the year. Payments made in advance are virtually the same as loans, but without interest. If an employee leaves during the year the unearned part of the pay increase is deducted from any pay or benefits due to the employee.

Advantages of Large-Sum Payments

A large sum can be used for a major purchase. This is beneficial to the employee. The employee (and family) will naturally think of the pay increase as worthwhile. The turnover of these people will probably be reduced as long as a significant portion of the "loan" is still unearned.

A large sum or periodic payment does not become part of the employee's week-to-week spending, whereas the 26 method means that the employee has a little more money to spend every two weeks. This spending will increase the employee's cost of living as well as standard of living. The employee and family become accustomed to this new, higher standard of living, so the benefit of the pay increase doesn't become notable. As a result, employees become dissatisfied with their pay again very soon.

Another advantage of permitting employees to decide how and when they will receive annual increases is that the employee, not management, has made the decision. This helps to satisfy a need for self-determination.

Pay Plans

Wage and salary scales designed by management are often misunderstood by employees. The more complicated the pay of course, the less the scales are understood.

Some small organizations or a department of a large organization have experimented with having employees design their own pay system.

A cleaning-service company had problems with employee attendance. The company asked the employees to collectively design a reward system for good attendance. Management was pleasantly surprised with the results. The employees carefully thought out a plan: the bonus to be paid was a conservative amount of money, much less than the cost to the company of non-attendance. Attendance improved significantly because the employees had designed the plan and were committed to making it successful.

But can employees effectively decide how much they and their fellow employees should be paid? Organizations are concerned that the interests of the employees will run counter to the interests of the organization. In one manufacturing organization, for instance, the employees function as work teams. Each work team is trained to perform five different jobs. New employees join a team and are trained by the other team members. The other team members decide collectively when the new employee should be upgraded into a higher job classification. The employee receives a pay increase when upgraded.

It Doesn't Always Work Most managers are opposed to allowing employees to participate in making decisions about pay. Except for simple plans, employees might lack the education, training, and experience needed to make an objective decision about their own pay.

Pay and Motivation

If pay is to be a motivator, performance and pay must be related. Employees also know what system will work best—and the best system should have the employees' input. Experience proves that when employees are trusted and given responsibility, they respond in a trustworthy and responsible manner.

FRINGE BENEFITS

A fringe benefit is an indirect form of compensation for employees.

Why should an employer provide these benefits? Here are some reasons:

1. The employer is concerned about the welfare of the employees.
2. Some benefits are legal requirements.
3. Collective bargaining and union pressure.
4. Competition from other employers.
5. Tax advantages for both the employer and employee.
6. Benefits might increase productivity and employee satisfaction.

If you are providing fringe benefits or planning to, you will probably find that many employees don't know what benefits they are receiving, or for what purpose. Employees also look on benefits as "rights" and not something to be earned. Benefits are not considered an important part of the employee's compensation. Benefits are lumped together as deductions such as income tax whose only purpose is to reduce gross income. Few employees consider the value of fringe benefits when considering take-home pay.

You, the employer, should have a policy on fringe benefits. Your policy could be one or more of the following:
1. Pay the legal minimum.
2. Do what competitors do.
3. Use benefits as monetary motivators.

First, check the legal requirements, which involve Unemployment Insurance, Workmen's Compensation, Canada Pension Plan, vacations and holidays, and health insurance. Some of these benefits are paid exclusively by the employer; others are shared costs.

Second, what other benefits should you consider? Benefits that exceed the legal minimum requirements are pension, vacations, health insurance (medical, dental, long-term disability), and life insurance.

Third, here are other benefits:
1. Supplementary unemployment income
2. Severance and termination pay
3. Profit sharing or bonuses
4. Stock purchase plans
5. Off-the-job education and training
6. Recreation facilities and programs
7. Cafeteria facilities
8. Subsidized coffee and meals
9. Discounts on merchandise and services
10. Employee savings plans and credit unions
11. Group car insurance
12. Parking
13. Lottery tickets

In addition to your policy on what benefits to provide, you will have to decide how much to pay and how much the employees should pay.

Sometimes competitors, unions, and employee pressure will influence your decision. Some wealthy and philanthropic organizations volunteer to pay 100%. Other organizations provide services at cost which is a lower price than the employees would have to pay on their own. Also, some fringe benefits may be low in cost but high in prestige—for instance, job titles and calling cards or anything enhancing the employee's feeling of status.

In addition to the direct cost of these benefits, you have an administration cost. This cost is usually proportionately higher for smaller organizations. However, you can minimize costs by combining benefit plans with other organizations.

Benefits as Motivator

It is difficult to relate fringe benefits to employee productivity and job satisfaction. The most that can be said with certainty is that fringe benefits will contribute to the image that your organization is a good place to work.

This image will attract prospective employees, reduce employee turnover, favourably influence suppliers, customers, and governments. You can conduct your own motivation survey by answering this question: of all the fringe benefits of all organizations, how many can be enjoyed on the job?

Your answer will probably be: None! The employee has to leave work, become unemployed, get hurt or sick, take a holiday, go to school, play hockey, retire, die, or whatever else the benefit is supposed to provide. Stock-purchase plans and profit sharing may be motivators, but only if the employees think of themselves as part-owners in the business.

Because benefits can cost 30% of your total payroll, you should plan to get a better return on your investment. Here are two ways:
A. Publicize the Benefits Make certain employees know the reasons for the benefits and their costs and how the benefits can be used. And don't assume that, once employees know the why and how of the benefits, they will continue to remember and understand. Your internal communications should be continuing. You have a selling job to do, just as you would expect for your sales force, advertising, and public-relations campaign.

Your communication campaign can consist of meetings; booklets; quarterly, semi-annual, and annual written reports; letters and reports mailed to employee's home; and copies of bills paid or benefits received. Every effort should be made to ensure that all employees know how they will benefit or how another employee has benefited.

B. Employees' Participation in Deciding Benefits The employees' perceptions of their needs could differ from the employer's perception of their needs. People are not stupid: they make well-thought-out decisions, especially on matters in their own interest.

You, the employer, should supply the employees with all the necessary information needed for deciding which benefits are best. First, give information on legal requirements. (See Exhibit 6-1; make sure that you know the provincial and federal requirements.) Second, show how these legally required benefits could be supplemented. (See Exhibit 6-2.) The benefits and costs are often based on the employee's income and the sharing of the costs between employer and employee.

Employees tend to be more interested in shared costs than in employer-paid benefits; free benefits are not motivators: employees tend to see these benefits as rights, not incentives.

Also, think carefully before you put items on the list for the employees' consideration. You may have difficulty withdrawing a benefit without the employee's acceptance.

Examples of benefits options are:

Life insurance could be available in multiples of $10,000, $20,000, and so on; equivalent to one year's income, two years' income, etc.; or a minimum lump sum, say $50,000. Pensions can be based on a percentage of each employee's income. Length of vacations could be an arbitrary decision by the employer. Provincial regulations may give the employee one week's vacation after one year of employment. You could add a second week for a one-year employee and a third week for a five-year employee.

Whatever you do, consider these guidelines:

1. Only give employees a choice if you want them to have a choice.
2. Only show a few choices under each category. Three choices should be a maximum.
3. Keep the terminology simple and clear.

But what will you do if the employees can't agree collectively? You can use the democratic method and accept the majority's choices. Or you can use the cafeteria method, so called because it is a pick-and-choose method of deciding on benefits.

In the cafeteria style, you tell employees how much you are willing to contribute to benefit plans in addition to the legal requirements. This contribution could be expressed as a percentage of the employee's annual income. The employee then

Exhibit 6-1

Fringe Benefits Required By Law

Benefits	Costs To	
	Employer	Employee
1. Unemployment Insurance	$	$
2. Workmen's Compensation		
3. Canada Pension Plan		
4. Holidays		
5. Vacations		
6. Health Insurance		
7.		
Total	$	$

Exhibit 6-2
Fringe Benefits
Voluntary Supplements to Legal Requirements

Benefits	Costs To	
	Employee	Employer
1. Pension	$	$
2. Vacations		
3. Life Insurance		
4. Medical Insurance		
5. Dental Insurance		
6. Long-term Disability		
7.		
Total	$	$

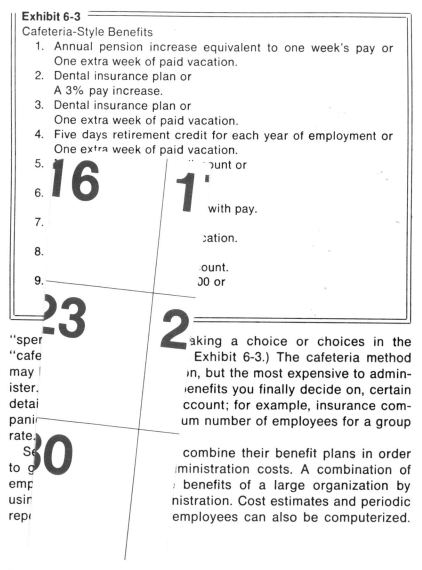
"sper
"cafe   aking a choice or choices in the
may   Exhibit 6-3.) The cafeteria method
ister.   ɔn, but the most expensive to admin-
detai   ienefits you finally decide on, certain
panir   ccount; for example, insurance com-
rate.   um number of employees for a group

Se   combine their benefit plans in order
to g   iministration costs. A combination of
emp   i benefits of a large organization by
usir   nistration. Cost estimates and periodic
rep(employees can also be computerized.

NON-FINANCIAL REWARDS

To understand the importance of non-financial rewards you have
to understand the needs of people. Most persons want to be
with other people. Very few want to be hermits. Even the person
who wants to work alone wants to know that there are other
people nearby. Others have a greater need to socialize on the
job. These people want jobs that bring them into direct and

continuing contact with people, whether employees, customers, or the public.

You have to accept social needs as legitimate, not as something that interferes with the day's work. Most employees spend more time with their fellow employees on the job than they do with their friends and family off the job. Employees want to have a feeling of belonging and acceptance. The employee who is accepted and has a sense of belonging will be more interested in going to work in order to enjoy the interpersonal relations that bring satisfaction.

Another important need is to have a "good boss." The boss must find out the individual needs of the employees, then treat those individuals as each wants to be treated. Neither task is easy. Some employees want a tough boss. Others want one who is firm but fair. And others want one who shares the decision-making process.

Not only do employees have individual preferences, but these needs could also vary with different work situations. What should a manager do? Get to know your employees so you can determine their individual needs, for one thing; this is an on-going and never-ending process. Also, be flexible in your supervisory style in accordance with individual needs, but be consistent in your supervisory style with each individual employee.

The better you are at knowing how to treat your employees, the more effective you'll be as a supervisor. Also, the employer-employee relationship will be more satisfying to both parties. Being flexible doesn't mean that you have to change your personality. You can be firm and still be friendly; you can be decisive and still be polite. You can give someone more freedom without giving away the company. The consistency of your style will depend on the consistency of the work situation. Effective leadership is situational: at times, you'll have to treat employees as a group rather than as individuals; the needs of the situation should dictate your leadership style.

There will also be situations where the needs of the organization supercede the needs of individuals or the group. When this happens, the employees' acceptance of the organization's needs will depend on how effectively you have established interpersonal relations with your staff. Employees also receive non-financial rewards when their ego needs are satisfied. Everyone wants a feeling of importance. This feeling can come from satisfaction on the job. It can also come from recognition by others of the importance of an employee. This recognition can come from the manager and fellow employees.

Status symbols are also important to many people: make a list of how you can satisfy your employees' needs for status:

_____

_____

Some people get rewards by being creative and having a sense of achievement. They want a job that permits self-fulfillment. But getting paid for self-fulfillment isn't always possible. That's why this need is not often satisfied.

In a previous chapter we discussed the advantages and disadvantages of working for your organization. That list will give you some ideas about the non-financial rewards offered by your organization. Non-financial rewards give a manager opportunities for attracting and keeping good employees. And you won't have to spend money for these rewards.

WHY IS BOWLING FUN?

The bowler has a visible goal. The goal is challenging. The goal is attainable. The bowler sets a personal performance objective. Since the bowler has little hope of a perfect score, a goal is set that can be reached or exceeded. If the objective was a perfect score, the bowler would go home frustrated. The bowler gets immediate feedback on the performance.

The bowler is a member of a group: as well as enjoying bowling, the bowler can satisfy social needs. If the bowler does well, satisfaction as well as recognition from the group result.

Now let's make some changes in the game.

Eliminate the pins. The bowler is now rolling a ball down an empty alley. What effect will this change have on the description above? What has happened to the goal? the challenge? the performance objective? the self-satisfaction? the recognition?

Leave the pins, but hide them with a curtain suspended from the ceiling about halfway down the alley. What will be the effects of this change? What has happened to the goal? the challenge? the performance objective? the satisfaction? the recognition? the feedback?

Eliminate the pins and add a person to tell you, the bowler, how well you are rolling the ball down the empty alley. This person will give you constructive criticism on the way you stand, the way you hold the ball, and how well you roll the ball. You might hear some comments on your personality, your attitude, your clothes, or your hair styles.

When the curtain is used, this extra person will stand so he can see which pins you have hit. He will tell you how well you have been doing and suggest how you might improve.

With the changes suggested in the previous two paragraphs, who will receive the credit if you do well and the blame if you do poorly? If you succeed, it's assumed that you followed directions and did what you were told to do. The person who gave directions receives credit. If you fail, it's assumed that you didn't do what you were told.

In order for you to perform better, this extra person will provide you with good bowling shoes, piped-in music, and cushioned seats when you are waiting for the ball to be returned.

It has been noted that when you are not bowling you're talking to other team members. To minimize this non-productive socializing, partitions have been built so that each person will be alone when seated.

Bowling is no longer fun. You will probably look for something else to do.

But wait!

The Bowling Company will pay you if you will roll the ball down the empty alley or down the alley that has the curtain. The hours are 9:00 AM to 4:00 PM. You will have an hour for lunch and a morning and afternoon coffee break. You will get sicktime credits, two weeks' holiday after one year and a nice pension at age 65. There is also the possibility of being upgraded from Bowler Class 1 to Bowler Class 4 with more pay and benefits. You could also be promoted to be a Bowling Supervisor. How much money would you want to be a bowler?

If you did decide to continue to bowl under the above conditions, what would happen to your punctuality? attendance? How would you feel when you got up in the morning? Would you look forward to another day of bowling? How often would you phone in "sick"? If bowling now seems like work, how many jobs do you think are like this?

JOB ENRICHMENT

Job functions in organizations consist of these activities:

1. Planning: setting goals. These can be daily or longer-term goals. Goals should be expressed in terms of quality, quantity, cost and time.

2. Organizing: the use of people, machines, materials, and equipment. Organizing includes work layout, methods, schedules, systems, and personal assignments.

3. Staffing: (sometimes included under organizing) recruiting, selecting, inducting, training, motivating, promoting people. Establishing a system for rewards and punishments.

4. Controlling: getting feedback for comparing achievements with goals. Measuring (refer to the standards of quantity, quality, cost, and time); evaluating (how well were the goals achieved?); correcting (if necessary) the planning, organizing and staffing.

5. Directing: ensuring that the employees are working to achieve the organization's goals; using positive and negative discipline.

6. Producing the product or service: the actual doing of the work. This is the output for which the company will be rewarded so it can continue to produce a product or service.

Let's have another look at these 6 items. This time, ask yourself, "who is responsible for ——?" and write your answer. Show the job title, not the person's name.

In my organization, who is responsible for:
1. Planning? _____ (Job Title)
2. Organizing? _____ (Job Title)
3. Staffing? _____ (Job Title)
4. Controlling? _____ (Job Title)
5. Directing? _____ (Job Title)
6. Producing the product or service? _____ (Job Title)

In most organizations the first five functions are performed by managers and supervisors. The sixth item is a function of the employees or workers.

Job enrichment is a method of delegating some of the traditional management functions to the employees. But why should this be done?

There are persons who analyze work, suggest ways to simplify work, and determine the best methods for doing the work. These "job engineers" found that the best way to get a job done is to divide the job into small units so that each unit could be understood and to perform the job by doing the smallest unit in the most repetitive way.

The job engineers have done a superb job in analyzing and

simplifying the work to be done. The employee's job was simplified so it was easy to do and was made repetitive so the employee could become a specialist. Simplification and specialization have resulted in tremendous increases in productivity. Now many of these jobs are being performed by machines or a combination of machines and people.

Management determined that it is important to differentiate between planning a job and doing a job: planning and doing are separate functions. Management also decided that, since the functions were different, they should be performed by different people. So management has traditionally been responsible for the planning and organization of jobs and the workers have been responsible for producing the product or service. In order to ensure that the work was done satisfactorily, management also added the functions of controlling and directing.

Traditional View of Work

Management is responsible for:	Workers are responsible for:	Under the:
Planning	Producing	Directing and
Organizing	the product	controlling by
Staffing	or service	management

Job Enrichment View of Work

Every employee should be the manager (to some extent) of his or her own job.

In order to be a manager, the employee or work team must be given some authority and responsibility for setting goals, organizing the workplace and the methods of doing the work, checking and measuring their output, evaluating their output, and correcting their methods and efforts if necessary.

The objective is to make the job complete or whole. By enriching the job, the employees will be exercising self-determination, self-regulation, and self-control. The more that self-control is responsibly used by employees, the less that external control will be needed by management. The supervisor then becomes an adviser, a consultant, and a co-ordinator.

Job enrichment gives employees opportunities for obtaining a sense of achievement and recognition. The new job functions make the employee's job more challenging. When these functions are performed well, the employee will have a feeling of satisfaction.

Giving employees more control over their own work satisfies a need for self-determination and freedom. Self-determination will lead to commitment. And commitment will remove much of the alienation the employee feels because of the job and the employer.

The improvement in productivity under job enrichment is really the result of the removal of a detriment to productivity. Most employees are only partially employed: they could do more and better work if they wanted to. In addition to being physiologically underemployed, under traditional work methods most persons are also psychologically underemployed.

The Case of the K Company

K Company is a small Canadian manufacturing company. The main part of production consists of five large machines. Each machine is operated by a team of six employees and produces a complete unit of output. All the machines are operated independently of each other. The Production and Engineering Department had set a daily quota of 960 units of output for each machine. The employees were paid an hourly wage and a team bonus based on the quantity of output.

For six months, the production for all machines fluctuated between 500 and 600 units daily. Management was certain that production could be higher. But in spite of the bonus the teams were restricting their output.

At the end of the six-month period, the Production Manager participated in a seminar on motivation. As a result he decided to try an experiment in job enrichment. He explained to his top management what he planned to do and received permission to put the plan into effect.

He called the five work teams together and asked them to decide what the quota should be. The employees were suspicious at first.

EMPLOYEE: You will accept whatever quota we set?

MANAGER: Yes.

EMPLOYEE: What about the bonus?

MANAGER: The bonus system will be adjusted to reflect the new quota. I will guarantee that no team will earn less money if it continues to produce the same output as before. But if you produce more you will earn more.

Both the manager and the employees know that the new quota

would be less than 960. The manager was taking a calculated risk that the employees would set a realistic but challenging goal. Moreover, the Production Manager, his staff, and employees had a good work relationship. The K Company had a reputation for treating its employees fairly.

This attempt at Job Enrichment, although new to K Company, was accepted by the employees as being sincere and honest. The Production Manager left the five teams alone to decide collectively what the new quota would be. The employees agreed that the quota should be 800. The manager then adjusted the bonus so that all teams could earn as much as before and more if production increased.

The result? In less than one week, all teams were producing more than 700 daily. The first reaction came from the Payroll Department. They told the Production Manager: "Your payroll costs have jumped! What's wrong?"

"Nothing's wrong. Everything's all right." Then he explained what had happened.

Based on the previous average of 500 to 600 units, production had now increased by 17% to 40%. Although wage costs had gone up, unit costs had gone down. The increased production had come from the same machines and employees.

Before the Job Enrichment session, the K Company had planned to buy another machine and increase total production by 20%. The costs of the machine, installation, startup, and running until quality and quantity were satisfactory were estimated at between $50,000 and $100,000. Space would have to be found for the machine. Six new employees would have to be hired. The new employees would have to be trained. The new machine would need maintenance. Who should get the new machine—the new employees or one of the other work teams?

Because the present work teams had increased production, management decided not to buy the new machine. The higher production meant that the machines needed more maintenance. Occasionally a machine would break down or have to be stopped, but the repairs could be made quickly by the work team.

Because of the possibility of damaging the machine accidentally, repairs could only be made under the supervision of the Plant Engineer.

When a machine broke down, the work crew called their foreman, who called the engineer.

The Plant Manager decided to speed up the communications. He installed a telephone beside each machine. Each phone was directly connected to another phone in the engineer's office. This hot line was to be used only for repair calls.

What happened? Communications were speeded up and machine downtime was reduced. The employees felt a sense of importance because they could call the engineer directly. The foreman felt threatened because he was bypassed. The engineer felt a loss of status because he was now taking orders from employees.

The Production Manager learned that when you solve one problem you may be creating one or more other problems.

The Case of T Company

T Company had a team of women assembling a complex radar set. The Engineering Department had determined the methods and procedures to be used by the team when assembling the set and the break-even point, which was 100 assembly hours per unit. But the workers were not told what the break-even point was.

The team took 138 hours to assemble each unit and T Company was losing money. There were problems with absenteeism, turnover, and training time. The women made many trips to the health centre. They also had many complaints, particularly about the quality of the food in the cafeteria.

Goal-Setting Session No. 1 At this point, the supervisor had a meeting with the team.

The team was shown the government contract for the radar set. They saw the terms of the contract, the dollar value, delivery schedules, and so on. They were shown T Company's costs for materials, labour, and related items.

The supervisor then asked the team to examine the method of assembly and suggest improvements as well as to determine how many hours would be needed to assemble the set.

The engineer and manufacturing staffs and inspectors were made available as a resource. They did not participate in the meeting and only supplied information when asked. During a two-hour meeting the team decided on new methods of assembling the set and that they could assemble it in 86 hours.

During the next two months, the team used its own methods and steadily reduced the assembly time to 75 hours.

Goal-Setting Session No. 2 One of the employees suggested that they should have another meeting. But the supervisor was excluded from the meeting. The women said she wasn't needed. The team decided to make more changes in the method of assembly and to set a new goal of 65 hours. During the next three months the assembly time was reduced to 57 hours.

Goal-Setting Session No. 3 At this meeting the target was set at 40 hours. During the next four months the actual assembly was reduced to 41 hours. In addition to greater productivity, other benefits resulting from these meetings were less absenteeism, lower turnover, fewer trips to the health centre, and fewer complaints about the cafeteria.

Job Enrichment The work team had accepted responsibility for planning, organizing, and controlling their work as well as doing the assembly. The idea to give the actual workers these responsibilities spread to other work groups and departments. The results were favourable and the company was able to obtain more government contracts.

The supervisors in these departments felt uncomfortable and threatened. Non-management people were doing management work. So the supervisors decided to have a meeting to discuss and define the new role of a supervisor. The result of this and other meetings helped to formulate a concept for a new supervisory role.

Old Role	New Role
1. Set goals for subordinates. Define standards and the results to be expected.	1. Participate with employees in setting goals or allow them to set their own goals.
2. Determine the methods for doing the job.	2. Allow employees to determine their methods and improvements.
3. Check employee's performance.	3. Let employees monitor their own performance.
4. Discipline employees.	4. Encourage and permit employees to use self-discipline.
5. Motivate employees by using leadership and persuasion.	5. Self-discipline and self-control minimize the need for direct supervision.
6. Be responsible for rewards and punishments.	6. Recognize the achievements of employees. Help them to learn from their mistakes.

Direct control by supervisors was replaced with functions of co-ordination, counselling, and training. The biggest task of the supervisor was to remove roadblocks so employees could get on with the job. These roadblocks could be caused by machines, equipment, materials, human problems, co-ordination with other jobs and departments, paperwork, communication, and so on. The supervisor becomes a resource because of knowledge, experience, and ability to teach. The supervisor supplies advice and encouragement and solves problems when necessary. Also, the supervisor accepts responsibility for the work of subordinates, thereby retaining the formal authority and power of a managerial position.

Will Job Enrichment Work in Your Organization?

Whether or not job enrichment will be successful in your organization will depend on the nature of management, the nature of the employees, and the nature of the job.

Do management and employees work in an environment where people have been or are encouraged to accept responsibility for self-determination, self-regulation, and self-control? Are work procedures loosely defined? Is the work situation unpredictable? Is there a degree of risk and uncertainty in determining the output?

Or are jobs clearly and precisely defined? Do managers and employees have little or no autonomy? Are jobs and people programmed to fit the technology of the organization? Is the output of the work situation predictable? Do people work for the system (organization) or does the system (organization) work for the people?

Summary:

1. Employees have the ability to improve their jobs.
2. Employees want to get satisfaction from their work.
3. Self-controlled change is motivational.
4. Employees satisfy social needs through group participation.
5. The supervisor must be supportive in the role of advisor and helper.

Job Enrichment Exercise

1. Select a job in your department or organization.
2. Make a list of the duties, responsibilities, or job functions.

(This information should be on an up-to-date job description).

3. Consider the functions of: planning, organizing, and controlling.
4. How can this job be enriched? Be specific. (Use Exhibit 6-4.)
5. Review the new job description: Is the job more complete? Is the job more challenging? Does the job have opportunities for self-determination? self-regulation? self-control? Is there less external control (close supervision)? Is the employee the manager of the job?
6. Select an employee and a work situation where you think the application of Job Enrichment will have a high opportunity of success.
7. Apply the Job Enrichment techniques to the employee and the job you have selected.
8. Follow up as an adviser, a consultant, and a teacher. Give encouragement.
9. Give recognition for success to the employee.
10. If the job-enrichment experiment isn't successful, accept your share of the blame.
11. Try again to make the job-enrichment experiment successful (or more successful).

Alternative:

Permit the employees or work group to do their own job-enrichment analysis. Giving an employee or employees this responsibility will depend on the type of work to be done, the skill and knowledge of the employee(s), and the willingness of the employee(s) to accept this new responsibility.

By permitting an employee to enrich the job, you are making use of the worker's knowledge and experience. Experience shows that an employee will set a higher personal goal, then reach or exceed that goal.

Management should reserve the right to modify that goal. In the case of T Company, the work group set their third goal at 40 hours, but the best assembly time was 41 hours. Management should have realized that 41 hours may have been the best that was possible. A goal better than this would depend on new methods of assembly.

If management finds that the team cannot reduce the time below 41 hours, they could arbitrarily set an optimum time of

45 hours. The team might insist they can do better than this time, but management should say, "Your performance has been exceptional. We are certain that you will continue to try to exceed your previous goals. But you are human. And there will be fluctuations in your performance. We will be satisfied if you assemble the unit in 45 hours or less."

Because workers set more difficult and challenging goals for themselves than management usually does, they sometimes set unrealistic goals which lead to frustration and disappointment. Management should determine through the workers' experience that the goals are realistic. The employees may have overcommitted themselves: workers won't reduce their goals and lose face, so management should make the decision for them.

Exhibit 6-4
Job Enrichment Worksheet

    A. Job _____

    B. Duties, functions, responsibilities:
       1. _____
       2. _____
       3. _____
       4. _____
       etc. _____
          _____

    C. New specific responsibilities for:
       1. Planning: _____
          _____
          _____

       2. Organizing: _____
          _____
          _____

       3. Controlling: _____
          _____
          _____

7

PEOPLE PROBLEMS AND HOW TO SOLVE THEM

DISCIPLINE

What is discipline? Discipline is not just punishment; discipline means to instruct, regulate, govern, chastise, and punish. Note that "punish" comes last.

Discipline begins with instructing subordinates in what to do and how to do it. The basis for all discipline is in having subordinates know right from wrong and what the supervisor expects.

The supervisor should emphasize the positive side of discipline. What are the rewards for the subordinate? Possible rewards include good treatment from the supervisor, praise, recognition, security, freedom from fear, upgrading, merit increases, promotion, voluntary overtime, and better job assignments.

Most employees want to and try to do a good job; only a small percentage of people usually cause most of the problems. Do you treat all of your employees as if they belonged to that small percentage? If you do, it won't be long before the minority becomes a majority. The supervisor is then the victim of self-fulfilling prophecy: what you expect from people is what you get.

A supervisor should set a good example. Do your rules apply to you as well as your subordinates? What about your own lateness, absenteeism, coffee breaks, lunch hour, personal use of the phone, and so on? "Do as I say, not as I do" may be a fringe benefit for supervisors, but a poor attitude toward discipline.

The goal of a supervisor should be self-discipline by employees. When employees discipline themselves, the supervisor doesn't have to be present for productivity to continue at an efficient level. According to the old saying, "If people only work when the boss is around there's something wrong with the boss."

Persons who do not respond satisfactorily to instructions must be controlled and corrected. The supervisor's attitude and actions should be "I want to help," rather than "I will punish you."

Before you decide on a course of action (or inaction), you should have answers for the questions. First, what are the rules for rules? (See Exhibit 7-1 for some suggestions.) Second, how should you enforce rules? (See Exhibit 7-2 for the Pot-Bellied-Stove method.) And third, how should you punish someone?

For this third question, consider the personality and attitude of the employee. What is your own attitude? Do you want to help or punish someone? Get the facts—All the facts, then verify them.

Exhibit 7-1
Rules for Rules

1. Does the rule have a purpose?
2. Is this purpose realistic?
3. Does everyone affected know the purpose?
4. Does everyone affected know the rule?
5. Does everyone affected understand the rule?
6. Are there penalties for not obeying the rule?
7. Are the penalties being enforced?
8. Do the persons concerned consider the penalties to be fair? too light? too severe?
9. Are the persons affected reminded of the rule periodically?
10. Should some persons formerly affected be freed from the rule?
11. Should the rule be extended to cover other persons?
12. Can the rule be complied with under present circumstances?

Exhibit 7-2
The Pot-Bellied Stove

1. You can see it's hot: everyone knows the rules.
2. If you touch it, without delay or indecision you will get burned: break rules—fast reaction from supervisor.
3. Same reaction every time you touch it: consistent punishment.
4. Same result no matter who touches it: no favouritism, impersonal.
5. The stove does not apologize for its action or become emotional or allow personal feelings to mix with disciplinary action. Doesn't make "example" of someone it doesn't like.

Let the employee tell his or her side of the story fully in a private interview. Be tactful. Don't belittle the other person. Don't become emotional; don't discriminate or let someone's personality affect your decision.

The supervisor is responsible for setting the disciplinary climate in the department. The climate or psychological environment results from the supervisor's actions. What does the supervisor emphasize or de-emphasize? What does the supervisor reward or punish? Or ignore? What does the supervisor watch closely and what indifferently?

Many managers and supervisors are not aware of how they cue employees to what is worth doing and what is not. An employee's performance will be shaped by these positive and negative reinforcements. Ask yourself what your action (smiles, frowns, and so on) or inaction is communicating in terms of what is relatively most important to you and what is secondary or even of no importance.

The employee decides what is worth doing, what is better ignored, and what should be avoided at all cost from cues taken from the supervisor. The employee's experience speaks louder than the supervisor's printed or oral instructions. Even so, nothing the supervisor does can be ignored, especially if either the employee or boss is new. The worker is looking for hidden cues to what is appropriate.

The Law of Effect says that:

1. Behaviour which proves rewarding will be repeated.
2. Behaviour which is punished tends not to be repeated.

It may be true that people who are rewarded will continue to do the same thing. But people who are punished could become unpredictable. The employee's reaction could be positive or negative.

Summary

1. Develop a feeling of mutual respect between yourself and your employees.
2. Train employees how to do their jobs efficiently and safely.
3. Keep employees satisfied with their jobs by effectively managing your human resources.

PROBLEM EMPLOYEES

What are the problems you and other employers have had with employees? Here are some that could be on everyone's list: absenteeism, lateness, alcohol, drugs, discipline, grievances, accidents, theft, moonlighting, gambling, and personal. What others have you had? _____

Before we try to solve some of these problems, let's first look at the Discipline Worksheet. (See Exhibit 7-3.) To get the most out of this chapter you should complete the Worksheet now. After you finish it, continue reading.

Read on *after* you have completed Exhibit 7-3.

What is the relationship between the rules which employees obey or disobey and the rules which the supervisor rewards, punishes, or ignores? The supervisor determines the psychological climate. And this climate or psychological environment results from the supervisor's actions. What does the supervisor emphasize or de-emphasize? What does the supervisor watch closely? indifferently? Supervisors, intentionally or unintentionally, indicate to employees what is worth doing and what is not. An employee's behaviour will be shaped by the positive and negative reinforcements of the supervisor. Each employee learns from experience. And each employee's attitude will reflect the supervisor's actions rather than rules printed in a booklet.

Why do employees break rules? Here are some reasons:
They don't like the rule.
They don't like the supervisor.
They don't like the organization.
They want to show off.
They have personal problems.
They respond to group pressure.
They ignore safety in order to get more productivity.
They are bored or frustrated.
They are jealous or angry because they weren't promoted.
The rule isn't clear or it's too complicated.

What are the causes of poor discipline? Does the supervisor obey the rules? Does the supervisor have too many subordinates? Is the supervisor an effective communicator? Does the supervisor show favouritism? Are employees rewarded for breaking rules?

Exhibit 7-3

Discipline Worksheet

Do each item in sequence. Don't read ahead.
1. List the orders (rules) in your organization or department in the order of acceptability by employees.
   a. Clearly acceptable. Are being obeyed willingly.

   _____

   b. Neutral. Barely acceptable or barely unacceptable.

   _____

   c. Clearly unacceptable. Are not being obeyed.

   _____

2. Which of the rules in your organization or department do you reward? punish? ignore? (Put the letters R, P or I opposite the items in No. 1.)
3. What is the relationship between No. 1 and No. 2 above?

   _____

4. Why do employees break rules?

   _____

5. What are the causes of poor discipline?

   _____

6. How should you discipline employees?

   _____

7. Should your objective be to punish a particular violation or to avoid future trouble? Why?

   _____

8. What favourable results have you had from any of the penalties you have imposed? Give examples.

   _____

9. How can you enforce rules by using self-discipline among employees?

   _____

   _____

Which rules does the supervisor reward, punish, or ignore? Does the supervisor use positive and negative reinforcement?

How should you discipline employees? The pot-bellied-stove idea is one method. But are there exceptions to every rule. What happens if an employee touches the stove accidentally? It wasn't the employee's fault. Why should the employee be punished? When you discipline:

1. Consider the personality and attitude of the employee.
2. Consider your own attitude. Do you want to help or punish the employee?
3. Get all the facts about the problem.
4. Interview the employee privately.
5. Let him tell his story fully.
6. Don't belittle the employee.
7. Verify information.
8. If you are wrong, admit it.
9. If you are partially to blame, share responsibility.
10. Discipline what the person has done and not who the person is.
11. Be fair. Don't discriminate or show favouritism.
12. Be tactful, constructive, and unemotional.
13. Be decisive.
14. Don't hold a grudge.

Is your objective to punish an employee or to prevent the incident from happening again? Punishment is a form of revenge —it hurts. But the punishment might act as a deterrent. Make the punishment fit your objective and make certain the employee knows your objective. Also, take into account whether the employee was careless when performing the duties or needs more training.

How can you use self-discipline to enforce rules? For example, a group of office employees had a 10% absentee rate. (Out of 20 working days in a month, each employee was away an average of 2 days.) The office manager had a meeting with all the employees in the department to show them the absentee records, but no names were mentioned. The manager asked them to set a target for acceptable absenteeism, then left them alone while they had their own meeting. The group set a target of not more than 3%, or one-half day a month.

The manager accepted the target. Because the target was self-imposed, the 3% was acceptable to the employees. Any employee who exceeded the target without good reason knew that discipline would be forthcoming.

This same idea can be used for lateness. Another method is to work through the informal group leader or the union steward. Employees using peer pressure can often apply more effective discipline than a supervisor can.

ABSENTEEISM

Why don't employees come to work? Some employees are absent because they're actually ill, but four types of absentees aren't ill at all. Here are some reasons (and suggested solutions) for these kinds of absenteeism:

The chronic absentee wakes up, looks at the clock, and thinks, "I'll never make it on time." So the chronic absentee has someone else phone in an excuse: this employee is not sick at all, but just wants a day off. The chronic absentee accounts for the highest percentage of absenteeism. This person probably had the same habits while attending (or not attending) other jobs. This person can't take the pressure, tires easily, and easily becomes frustrated; little obstacles become big difficulties. So the chronic absentee becomes convinced that he or she is sick—too sick to go to work.

Suggested Solution: Don't ask the employee the reason for the absence. Just tell the employee the consequences or effects of the absence: "We sure missed you. We kept getting behind in the work. We depended on you to be here."

The escapist absentee is having problems with the job. Wouldn't it be nice to do something else? "Maybe I'll take tomorrow off." This employee could also be underused or finds the job boring. And tomorrow, as planned, the escapist phones in with an excuse for not coming to work.

Suggested Solutions: Check this employee's attendance record. The employee might have a pattern of taking a day off now and then, but might not be aware of the record. Talk to the employee about the job and the problems the employee might be having. Threatening with punishment won't solve the problem. Instead, ask, "Who can take your place when you're not here?" Discuss the rewards of regular attendance and the affect on the employee's career: "I can only give more responsibility or a promotion to the person who deserves it. What does your record show?" The only permanent cure might be to give the employee a more challenging job.

The immature absentee looks on work as a game played for

fun and not taken seriously: "It doesn't really matter if I work or not." "Everyone else takes time off." "Management expects someone to be absent." "I'm entitled to some time off." Immature, by the way, doesn't necessarily mean young.

Suggested Solutions: Show the employee the attendance record. "Absenteeism is not a fringe benefit. It's for things like illness." "You're no longer in school. You are doing important work. You have responsibilities to yourself, your fellow employees, and the organization. We had to pay overtime because you were absent."

The rehearsed absentee goes to the supervisor with a well-rehearsed speech which you've heard before: "My kid is sick and I have to go home" or phones in and says, "My doctor says I'm too sick to come to work." This person may not have a happy supervisor-employee relationship and the supervisor knows it. The employee quotes rules and demands rights. The request for time off is sometimes used as an excuse to have an argument.

Suggested Solutions: Be firm. "You do good work when you're here, but you've been away five times because of your child. If I can't rely on you, I'll have to get someone else. But I think you can control your absenteeism." Another line runs, "The letter from your doctor doesn't impress me. I'm getting used to seeing these. When the illness is minor, it's usually the patient and not the doctor who decides if you go to work."

The legitimate absentee phones the supervisor and says, "I twisted my leg. I can hardly walk but I'll try to get in later." The supervisor replies, "Don't try to come in. Take it easy. I'll see you tomorrow." But how can you tell if the employee is telling the truth?

This employee is rarely absent, usually the one with a cold or 'flu who comes to work instead of staying home. Snowstorms and car breakdowns don't stop this employee. Unforeseen circumstances might cause the employee to be late but rarely absent.

Suggested Solution: Treat the absenteeism as legitimate.

Summary

1. Enforce the rules. Treat everyone the same. Don't show favouritism. If you don't enforce the rules you will increase the possibility of more absenteeism.
2. Keep records. Who was absent and why?
3. Be realistic. You can reduce absenteeism, but not eliminate

it. Employees might consider minor absenteeism as a non-financial reward.

4. Efforts to reduce absenteeism are worth your time and effort. The indirect cost of absenteeism is four or five times more than the direct cost.

5. The real reasons for absenteeism are often directly related to job status, to work satisfaction, and to the way an employee is treated by the supervisor and fellow employees.

LATENESS

Why are some people always on time and some are consistently late? The three general causes are the conditions controlled by the supervisor or management, the conditions controlled by the employee, and the conditions over which the employee has no control.

Some of the controllable conditions involve how an employee feels about the supervisor and fellow employees, having more than one job at a time (moonlighting), alcohol and drugs, job dissatisfaction and working conditions, personal and family situations (domestic problems), overtime, and sleeping in.

Some of the uncontrollable conditions involve bad weather, the car-pool driver or public transit, illness (self and family), and accidents.

Lateness (and absenteeism) are usually caused by the work situation rather than the off-the-job situation. Moreover, usually a few people account for most of the problem. Lateness (and absenteeism) often decreases with age. Older workers generally have better records than young employees. The distance a person travels to work has little effect on punctuality. The rate of lateness goes up on Monday and the day after a holiday.

The employee has to decide on priorities. Is it easier or more important or rewarding to be late? Lateness can become a habit. The initial reason for being late has been forgotten or the condition no longer exists, but the employee continues to be late. The employer can combat lateness by making the work environment more psychologically rewarding. Employees want the security of good supervision, a feeling of belonging, a sense of pride and importance in the work itself, recognition for their efforts, and participation in making decisions that affect them. If the employer can satisfy these needs, employees could look forward to going to work every day instead of dreading—and therefore delaying—going to work. So the real reason for lateness is probably dissatisfaction with the job, the supervisor, or the other employees.

THEFT

Theft is wrong. Correct? Maybe not. Some organizations allow employees' theft as a means of reducing absenteeism and turnover and to provide job enrichment. (This is not a pun: the job enrichment refers to making a dull job more interesting as well as rewarding.) Petty theft is no longer considered a crime by some employers and employees; it is a fringe benefit. These employers find that theft amounts to about 5% to 8% of payroll costs.

An employer who reduces theft has to increase turnover. Before firing an employee for theft, you have to consider what it will cost to replace the employee, what it will cost in supervision to catch the thief, and what it will cost in equipment (TV cameras) to monitor what employees are doing.

To motivate employees you have to enrich the job by making it more challenging and meaningful as well as having to pay more money so the employee will not quit. Many jobs are boring and repetitive. The employee turns to theft as a means of using creative ability and intellectual energy. The employee sets a goal and makes decisions which provide a reward.

One organization reduced theft to almost nothing, but found they couldn't attract applicants for dull and routine jobs. When theft was permitted but kept under control, applicants became available again and turnover dropped.

Many employees don't steal because they need what they take, but because they want to see if they "can beat the system." So don't make stealing easy: make the employee work at it.

The auditor of one company found that the bookkeeper was stealing $2000 a year. This was reported to the president who said, "I pay him $10,000, but he's worth $15,000. The bookkeeper takes the $2000 because it's tax free. He comes to work every day and he's on time. He never takes a day off or gets sick. I have a hard time getting him to take a holiday. The books are in excellent condition because he doesn't want anyone finding mistakes or interfering with what he does. He won't take too much or it would be noticed. He's a good bookkeeper—and cheap at the price."

Bonding

One small organization tells job applicants, "Our employees have to be bonded. The bonding company checks the background of each employee. They check a person's criminal record and financial situation. They check to see if a person is deeply in debt or is a gambler. Only those with a good background can be bonded. We need your permission before we let the bonding company do any investigating. If we hire you, will you agree to be bonded?"

The person who is hired is given the bond application to complete. Unknown to the employee, the employer puts the application on the employee's personal file without taking out a bond. The employer, then, leads employees to believe that they have been bonded.

The employer gives these reasons for bonding employees: "If you do anything dishonest, the bonding company will prosecute you. We are too small to chase after a dishonest employee and pay for prosecuting you. The bonding company is big enough to have its own investigators to track you down. They have no personal interest in you and will do anything they can to make you pay for being dishonest. All this will be on your record when you try to get another job." The employer hopes that the employee will be afraid to be dishonest. At the same time, the employer saved the cost of bonding employees.

The job applicant who does not want to be investigated will not want to be an employee of that firm and therefore decline employment there. The employer knows that those who agree to be bonded must have "nothing to hide." This method of screening saves the employer the time, trouble, and expense of checking the applicant's criminal record, financial background, and other personal data.

TURNOVER

Is turnover a problem in your organization? To reduce turnover, you first have to collect the facts. Use Exhibit 7-4 as a worksheet for determining turnover in your organization. The time period can be changed to three months or six months. Exhibit 7-5 is an attempt to collect more data about each person who left. Items 5 to 8 are meant to be objective. Under Item 5, put in details

Exhibit 7-4

One Year's Turnover _____ to _____

Job Function	A Number Employed 1 year ago	B How Many Have Left?	C % Turnover $\frac{B}{A} \times 100$

Managers (office):
  Upper
  Middle
  First-Line			

Managers (factory):
  Upper
  Middle
  First-Line			

Sales reps
Office:
  Administration
  Clerical			

Factory:
  Administration
  Clerical
  Technical			

Operators: skilled			
Operators: unskilled			
Total			

you think might be important for your organization and your employees. Exhibit 7-6 is a summary of the number of persons who left for various reasons.

In collecting data, you have to be as objective and accurate as possible; your interpretation of the data will probably be more subjective. For example, refer to Exhibit 7-5. Do you think there is any correlation between Item 4, Reason for quitting, and Item 5, Personal data? You have to be careful not to jump to conclusions. If 18-to-21-year-old male employees quit after three months, does it mean that you shouldn't hire more people with similar characteristics? Do you have more turnover among secondary-school graduates or non-graduates? Are married people more reliable than single? Does a person's previous job history tell you anything?

Exhibit 7-5
Turnover Worksheet No. 2

1. Employee's name _____ Date of termination _____
2. Job function _____
3. Reason for termination (circle one):
   quit, fired, laid off (no work), retired, ill health, accident, died.
4. Reason for quitting or firing:

Complete Items 5 to 8 for persons who quit or were fired.

5. Personal data:
   Age _____
   Sex: M or F
   Marital status (circle one):
      single, married, separated, divorced, widowed.
   Education (show last grade completed or number of years of college, university, trade school, or other pertinent educational data.)
   Training or qualifications: _____
6. How long employed? _____
7. Job history: Was this employee's first job? _____
   How long employed at other organizations? _____
8. Other data: _____
   _____

Don't worry if you can't come to any specific conclusions. The problem may not be obvious from the data. But don't blame your bad luck and don't be consoled because other organizations have similar problems. The problem may be caused by management and the conditions of work. New employees may be different from what you expect; the new employees' expectations may be different from what the job provides.

So let's look closer at what causes turnover and how turnover can be reduced. Most turnover occurs among young, unskilled persons who were high-school dropouts, mainly because they are often transient workers. Consequently, these young people do not identify with their employer any more than with the community where they live. Their period of employment is usually less than six months.

Young married employees can also have turnover. These young marrieds may have the desirable characteristics of wanting to establish a home and become part of a community. Then why do these people, who have an incentive to seek steady work, quit after a short stay? Often these young people are highly skilled

Exhibit 7-6

Turnover Planning Worksheet No. 3

Time period _____ to _____

Reasons For Leaving (show how many persons)

Job Functions (See Ex. 7-4)	Quit	Fired	Laid Off	Retired	Ill Health	Accident	Died
Total							

and educated. They have expectations of finding a job that will be interesting, a job that will require the use of their talents and potential. These young marrieds usually postpone becoming parents. Both seek employment so they can enjoy the good life; they have a desire for instant or near-term material success.

Both husband and wife want jobs they like to do. When both are employed, it's less risky for either one to quit a dull job while the other becomes the sole breadwinner. Whether married or single, many young people prefer to be unemployed rather than do a job they dislike. The problem, as one employer said, is, "No one starves anymore." Unemployment benefits, welfare, relatives, and friends make survival easier for the unemployed. If the social benefits of not working were removed, the unemployed might have a different attitude towards holding a job. But the alienation of the worker from the work or employer would remain.

The first six months of employment seem to be critical: those who stay the first half-year usually stay two or maybe three years before looking for another job. Organizations find that older workers provide stability in the work force. One distribution centre won't hire anyone under forty. The forty-year-old has to be physically healthy and have the strength to do manual labour. But with modern materials-handling equipment, people have few problems meeting performance standards. Because the over-forty worker has a hard time finding a job, this organization also finds that they have few problems with attendance and punctuality.

Another organization, a retailer, had problems getting young people to work on certain nights during the week. The young people did not want to work Friday and Saturday nights, so they were allowed to work other nights. The older, married employees were told to work Friday and Saturday nights. They grumbled and complained, but they worked the nights that were undesirable for young single employees. One oldtimer said, "Here I'm working while those young ones are off having a good time. Who's running this store anyway?" Young people, especially single ones, are more mobile than married and older employees. Those with attachments to families and physical possessions don't quit their jobs easily or quickly.

The period of orientation is critical for most employees. The new employee is confronted with many unknowns: the small organization may be unknown, the neighbourhood may be unknown, the job functions may be unknown, the boss may be unknown, and the other employees are unknown. Most employees don't look on these unknowns as an adventure to be looked forward to or as something stimulating or exciting. Therefore, the first day and week are often short-term determinates of longer-term attitudes and behaviour. But each person is an individual with different needs and characteristics. Some people are more tolerant of what they consider to be an unsatisfactory job or working conditions; others are happy with their job, their fellow employees, and their employer, but quit because they want a new environment.

One woman who was employed by a temporary-help agency performed two days of satisfactory work for an employer. When asked to work a third day she refused. "I never work more than two days in the same place. That's why I take temporary jobs." This is an extreme case of a satisfied worker constantly seeking a new environment and a new challenge. But she is an individual with her own needs.

Many organizations, large and small, have analyzed their turnover and concluded that a good person is hard to find and that a good person is hard to keep. The job market is large, but only a few persons have the desirable characteristics you want. But the desirable person might not find the same desirability in you, the job, or your organization.

One organization solved its problems of turnover among lower-level unskilled jobs. Out of a work force of about forty, they usually needed three employees every three or four months. Their advertisements in the paper attracted between seventy and one hundred applicants. Screening out those with undesirable characteristics reduced the list to about a dozen. Rather than spend time and money trying to pick three out of twelve, they arbitrarily chose six persons. The decision was subjective.

After three or four weeks on the job the supervisor knew which three to keep. The other three were terminated usually for justifiable reasons. By using this method of recruitment and on-the-job assessment, this organization now recruits about three employees twice a year. This turnover is now considered normal.

Some organizations bribe their employees to stay by paying incentives based on length of employment. These incentives are also paid to employees who recruit their friends. If friends stay a minimum period, the employees who recommended them receive a bonus. Pressure from fellow employees can be a powerful influence in persuading employees to stay or leave. These incentives are also used when an organization uses an employment agency, but the incentive is a negative one. If the new employee doesn't stay a minimum period, the agency refunds all or a portion of the placement fee.

Turnover Policy and Strategy

You should consider three things: recruitment policy and strategy, short-term retention policy and strategy, and long-term retention policy and strategy. All three are related problems. Because of its size, the management of a small business can integrate all three, rather than deal with each one separately.

1. Awareness of the Problem How important is the turnover problem? Use information from Exhibits 7-4 and 7-6 to help you decide whether turnover is increasing, decreasing, or remaining the same. Are certain job categories more affected than others? In assessing the problem, decide to what extent turnover is or was affected by the labour market and economic conditions. But be careful not to blame the problem on external rather than internal factors.

Be certain that all managers and supervisors are aware of the organization's data on turnover. In a small business, most managers and supervisors are directly involved in the recruiting and retention of employees. This involvement makes integration of turnover policies and strategies much easier.

2. Validate the Turnover Data A subjective decision will have to be made on the relevance of the information. Turnover should be classified under the categories of full-time employees, part-time employees, and temporary or seasonal employees. The characteristics of employees should be compared with the job specifications. Are you hiring the right people? What are the characteristics of those who leave and those who stay?

Compare the characteristics of those who stay with the desirable characteristics of the job specifications. What is the relevance between job specifications, the characteristics of recruits, and the characteristics of those who stay on the job? If you get through that analysis, you will then be able to answer one more question: how successful have you been in recruiting and retaining employees with desirable characteristics?

3. Analyze the Costs of Turnover Refer to the section on human-resources valuation and costs. The Replacement-Cost Worksheet will show you the net costs of replacing an employee. Use Exhibit 7-7 to record and collate the costs for your organization.

Exhibit 7-7

Costs of Turnover

Time Period _____ to _____

Job Functions (See Exhibit 7-4)	Turnover (how many?)	Cost per employee ($)	Total costs ($)
Total		$	$

Recruitment Strategy and Tactics

More effective recruiting will give you the quickest results in reducing turnover as well as the best foundation for short- and long-term retention. If you recruit the high turnover employees, you should expect high turnover. You have to take the time and effort to recruit according to your job specifications and to thoroughly perform all the steps in the recruiting process. If you do not follow your planned recruiting strategy and tactics, then you are trusting to luck in selecting suitable employees.

Perhaps you should set standards of performance for the person or persons responsible for recruiting. If so, what would the performance appraisal indicate?

There are always "good" reasons for not taking the time and effort needed in recruiting. Some of these reasons are:

There is a shortage of applicants. We have to take what we can get.

New employees are needed right away. Understaffing means less production.

They'll learn to like the job. We're a good organization.

The pay and benefits will be an incentive to do good work. Money is the motivator.

There is a surplus of applicants. Jobs are hard to find so turnover will be lower.

Our supervisors know how to manage all types of people.

She's married, has a family and a mortgage, needs a job, and we need her.

He's over forty. His job-hopping days are over.

These "good" reasons could result in higher induction and training costs, lower productivity, lower morale and dissatisfaction among your present employees, breakup or disruption of established work groups, more supervision, and higher turnover among your best employees.

One of the biggest induction problems is integrating the newcomer into established work groups. This is less of a problem when turnover is low. But, when turnover is high, the oldtime employees can become indifferent to newcomers. The newcomer perceives this indifference as being unfriendly. Your present employees might also feel that they are spending too much of their time training newcomers. A frequent complaint is, "I spend most of my time training new people. When am I supposed to get my work done? I should be paid extra for training, because it's not my job."

Short-Term Strategy and Tactics

A manager is responsible for physical assets—building, machinery, equipment, furniture, materials—as well as the maintenance and repair of these physical facilities. These facilities must be adequate and trouble-free to ensure their availability for optimum productivity.

Managers should have a similar attitude toward their human assets. Management's attitude and behaviour toward new employees is usually the single most important factor in influencing turnover. Therefore, people should be treated with care. Human assets are mobile: determination, two legs, and a few minutes and a human asset has left the job. If physical assets had the same mobility, managers would worry. But there are differences between physical and human resources. Human Resources are more difficult to replace, take longer to reach performance objectives, and cause greater interference with the organization's goals of production or service.

Attention to human assets should begin from the moment the applicant becomes an employee: the new employee is more likely to leave in the short term. The short-term employee has to be convinced that the advantages of staying are greater than the advantages of quitting.

The recruiter should not exaggerate or oversell the job, the working environment, and the employee's prospects. The new employee will be making a decision to stay based on first impressions. If the new employee finds less than expected, that first impression will create doubts about the decision to accept employment with your organization.

It is important that you keep your promises. Whatever the new employee was told would happen should happen. Management must establish credibility at the beginning. When you create a credibility gap, it is difficult and sometimes impossible to bridge that gap.

The care and attention given to human resources should never end. The manager or supervisor is responsible for continuing an ongoing program of care and understanding of each employee. Occasional mistakes by management are usually tolerated by satisfied employees. However, an employee's reason for leaving is often the result of a single incident caused by management.

Each person, as mentioned before, is an individual and has individual needs. It is the supervisor's job to be aware of these needs and to try and satisfy them, especially the non-monetary needs. Treat employees as individuals: an employee's name is more important than the personnel number; all employees performing the same job in the same department are individually different. Give praise and recognition informally and when deserved. Use positive discipline: the supervisor should encourage, help, and train the employee; the employee should have a sense of security and confidence in the future.

Desirable Turnover

In spite of the best recruiting, induction and training programs, and the efforts of supervisors, some employees should not be retained. Sometimes the employee realizes that a change is in order and quits. Other times management has to take the initiative and terminate the employee.

The main reasons for desirable turnover are that the employee is either non-productive or counterproductive, or the employee has poor interpersonal skills. In short, the employee's behaviour is disruptive.

Other employees usually know why someone has quit or been fired, but management should ensure that the reasons are communicated to other employees. Employees have a right to know, because their own well-being and future are involved; they want to make sure that management does not fire employees arbitrarily or on a whim. There are exceptions to this rule—for example, when the reasons for leaving are personal.

Long-Term Strategy and Tactics

Losing an employee after a year or two can be expensive, especially for skilled jobs or service occupations. By this time the employee should know the job well, having performed it under a variety of situations and circumstances. The employee has survived mistakes and crises, become a member of a well-knit work team, and proven to be reliable, dependable, and predictable. The organization's short- and long-term progress depends on the retention of employees like this.

But why should the employee stay? Whether or not an employee stays usually depends on money, career goals, and non-monetary rewards. The supervisor should be aware of any changes in the needs of individual employees.

How important is money? What new financial commitments has the employee made? or is planning to make? Is the employee planning to buy a house or a new car? send a daughter to university? or planning an overseas trip? This need for extra money may make the employee dissatisfied with present income.

How important is upgrading, transfer, or promotion? Some employees want a change through a transfer or job rotation. Not everyone can be given a title, but almost everyone can be given more responsibility.

How important is the feeling of belonging? Employees become psychologically attached to their employer, their job, their fellow employees, and supervisors. This emotional attachment makes changing jobs more difficult. The performance appraisal and salary review become more important to longer-term employees. The supervisor or manager who has a good day-to-day working relationship with the employees can privately have a heart-to-heart talk with them.

The purposes of these interviews should be to find out what is important to the employee and tell the employee what the company has to offer. The interviewer should be open, frank, and honest. For example, an employee who wants to be promoted should be told what the prospects are. The person who wants to be promoted but can't be doesn't necessarily quit. This employee could continue to be productive, while off the job receiving that "promotion" by working for a service club or a social organization. Management must also recognize when they are using short-term solutions for long-term problems. Dissatisfaction with pay can be solved by bribing employees to stay. But this is only a temporary solution. If management is unwilling or unable to pay more money regularly, the employee who wants more money will eventually leave.

As the needs of employees change, so do the organization's reward system. Pensions might be more important than pay raises. A lump-sum bonus to be spent on travel might be as important as an extra week's holiday. Titles might be as important (sometimes more important) than pay raises. Shares in the company can build long-term commitment. Steady employment during economic downturns is a reward for loyalty. Dental plans for the employee's children assume major importance for some married persons.

Compare the costs of replacing a long-term employee with

the costs of retention. You will have to ensure that the monetary and non-monetary rewards are satisfactory to both you and the employee.

8

SPECIAL SITUATIONS

In this chapter we look at flexible work hours for employees, job sharing, terminating employees, and collective bargaining.

FLEXIBLE HOURS

Flexible hours, also called flextime, allow employees to select their own starting times, lunch periods, and finishing times. Employees in a manufacturing company may, for example, start work anytime between 7 AM and 8 AM, take a one-hour lunch sometime between 11:30 AM and 1:30 PM, and finish their workday between 3:30 and 4:45 PM. The office workers in the same company may start anytime between 7:45 and 9 AM, have a one-hour lunch sometime between 11:55 AM and 1:25 PM, and finish work between 4 and 5:15 PM. Employees may select their own schedules, as long as they work eight hours each day. (The factory workers are unionized and the flexible hours were approved by the union.)

The employees of a small government office, as another example, may begin work between 7 and 9 AM, have a thirty-minute or one-hour lunch, and leave between 3:30 and 5 PM. Each employee must work seven-and-a-half hours each day. Those who start at 9 AM and take a one-hour lunch must work "overtime," but are not paid overtime rates.

As a third example, employees of an insurance company may start work between 7:30 and 10 AM, have a thirty-minute to two-hour lunch, and leave work between 3:30 and 6 PM. Each employee must work 135 hours a month. An employee may work an extra ten hours, which can count towards the next month's total, or ten hours less, in which case the deficit is added to the next month's total. The credit or deficit may not exceed 10 hours for one month.

Other organizations have variations of these flextime systems:

1. Extra hours, up to a maximum per day, may be accumulated so that the employee can take a half day or a full day off.
2. Manufacturing work teams must decide as a group what the hours for their team will be.

Advantages of Flexible Hours

The employee can see the immediate personal benefits. The benefits are clear and first hand, not remote. Employees gain control over an important factor—the use of their own time, thus filling the need for independence and freedom. The employee is treated like a responsible person, a person who can be trusted to make a decision of benefit both to self and organization.

Some organizations have had an increase in productivity: increases of 15% have been recorded; no organization reported that productivity was reduced. Personal activities are done on the employee's own time instead of during working hours. An employee can finish a job before leaving for the day: an employee working on fixed hours either wouldn't begin the job because there wouldn't be time to finish, or would start the job, stop at quitting time, and begin again the next day; either way, time is lost by not starting the job or trying to begin where you left off the previous day. This elimination of downtime can increase productivity.

When all employees arrive at the same time, the beginning of the work day is often spent on socializing. With flexible hours, employees arrive at different times and find others are already working. The new arrival usually begins work much sooner than under the traditional system. Fewer employees are at work at any one time during the flexible hours. An employee can concentrate more on work because of fewer interruptions from other employees. An employee can be at work when needed the most. Persons in sales or other public-contact jobs can be present during peak work demands. Employees in accounting, data processing, shipping and receiving, mail pickups and delivery, and so on also have peak demands during the day and certain days of each month.

Employees learn each other's jobs because someone has to fill in during employee absences. Skills are thereby transferred throughout the department and the organization. Employees improve their interpersonal skills. The result is better teamwork.

An employee can schedule arrival and departure times to miss rush-hour traffic jams. Less time is spent commuting and the employee arrives fresher and in a better mood each day. The only time employees are late is when they arrive after the flexible time period in the morning, something which rarely happens. Flexible starting times eliminate an employee's guilt feelings at being late and need for discipline by the supervisor. Absenteeism is also reduced, especially for personal matters. An employee who is absent for a minor illness usually returns faster because of the changed attitude toward the job.

Customer service may increase because employees are on the job during a longer work day. For example, customers and the public could be served from 7:30 AM to 6:00 PM.

Overtime is reduced, work hours count toward a maximum number of hours per week instead of per day, and the demand for machines, equipment, and other physical facilities is spread over a longer work day.

Flextime helps in recruiting employees.

Some people function better in the morning and others late in the day. The employee can pick work hours which are psychologically and physiologically compatible with personal peaks of productivity.

The role of the first-line supervisor changes. The supervisor spends less time disciplining employees and more time in planning, organizing, problem solving, coaching, training, and coordinating.

Disadvantages of Flexible Hours

There may be few employees working Monday morning and Friday afternoons. Customer service may suffer if key employees are absent and replacements have not been trained. Some types of work, especially in production, require everyone to be present so that the work is processed continuously. Flexible hours might result in bottle necks, shortages, and work pile-ups. There might be extra costs for lighting, heating, and security. Time-recording equipment may be needed and may remind employees of time clocks. Equipment can be leased or purchased for about $60 per employee.

Less overtime means less pay for some employees. Conversely, supervisors might have to work longer hours. Some work longer hours even if their presence is not needed. Some supervisors feel a threat to their jobs and status if they find employees can perform effectively without the supervisor being present.

Communication may suffer because the needed person is absent. Messages and memos pile up. Meetings can only be scheduled during the core period. In the same way, car pools may be affected.

Increases in productivity may be of short duration because the novelty effect of flexible hours may wear off. Government regulations and union agreements may prevent anyone from exceeding a certain number of working hours each day. Employees may want to and may need to exceed these maximums to build up a surplus or reduce a deficit.

Not all departments in an organization might be convertible to flexible hours. This means that some departments could be on flexible hours and some could not. This duality of working hours might have a negative effect on morale.

Summary

Fixed hours are often picked arbitrarily by management or by tradition and past practices, whereas Flextime permits employees to pick their own hours within reason. Flexible hours give lower-level employees in office and factory the freedom usually enjoyed by managers and professional people.

For most organizations, the advantages of flextime outweigh the disadvantages, particularly in jobs where productivity is difficult to measure—clerical, administrative, and service to customers and the public. White-collar jobs require more supervision than blue-collar jobs because blue-collar jobs are easier to measure in terms of productivity and easier to supervise since the tasks are more uniform and easier to oversee.

Flextime is an attempt to make every employee a manager—at least of time. Most employees respond by using self-direction for their job functions. Self-direction means less supervision is needed.

Case Studies

One small manufacturing company introduced flexible hours and gave a key to every factory worker. This key was necessary for the early arrivals and for those who locked up at the end of the day. Employees, even those who didn't use their keys, had a

Exhibit 8-1

Flextime Planning Worksheet

1. What hours do I have to be open? _____
2. What hours would I like to be open? _____
3. Legally what are the maximum hours a person may work each day? _____ Each week? _____
4. Should I let an employee accumulate extra hours? _____ If so, how many? _____
5. Will I have to pay overtime for these extra hours? _____
6. Should I allow employees to have a deficit of hours? _____ If so, how many? _____
7. Can I give keys to employees without worrying about security? _____
8. How will an employee's time be recorded? _____
9. Will employees be able to learn each other's job so they can cover times when someone is absent? _____
10. Do I have enough employees so that important job functions are always being performed by someone? _____
11. What can I do about Monday AM and Friday PM? _____
12. Will the work flow suffer (pile-ups and shortages)? _____
13. What will be the extra costs for lighting, heating, time recording equipment, keys, etc? _____
14. What will be the effect on:
    lateness? _____
    absenteeism? _____
    overtime? _____
    time off? _____
    sick time? _____
    turnover? _____
    morale? _____
    supervision? _____
15. Will managers and supervisors have to work longer hours? _____
16. Will I get more sleep or less? _____
    These are special considerations for my business:
17. _____
18. _____
19. _____
20. I will _____ will not _____ try flexible hours.

feeling of importance. Management was recognizing them as important people and people who could be trusted. Morale went up. The result? Productivity increased.

The biggest obstacle to flextime is the supervisor who feels obliged to be there to supervise people: "How can employees who are left on their own be expected to work?"

Thousands of organizations in North America and Europe have tried flexible hours. Employees are almost unanimous in praising the new system. Only a few organizations have returned to the traditional fixed hours.

Organizations that fear a loss of productivity because of a lack of supervision more than make up for an expected loss through savings in punctuality, absenteeism, time off, sick time, overtime, turnover, morale, and supervision. As one manager said: "If I can get all those benefits, I don't mind losing a little productivity." Exhibit 8-1 is a Flextime Planning Worksheet. Complete the Worksheet, then make your own decision on whether or not to adopt flextime for your organization.

JOB SHARING

Two persons perform the same job functions but at different times. They share the same work space, facilities, and salary. This system is also known as job swapping.

Here is an example: Two women share a clerical job. Woman 1 works Monday and Tuesday; Woman 2 works Wednesday, Thursday, and Friday. The next week Woman 2 works Monday and Tuesday and Woman 1 works Wednesday, Thursday, and Friday. The days of work can be varied to suit the needs of the job and the employees.

In another example, one employee works from 9 AM to 12:30 PM. The other person works from 12:30 PM to 4:00 PM. Another variation is to have one employee work a full week, another employee works the next week, and so on. Job swapping is used in all types of jobs: factory, clerical, machine operators, switchboard operator, secretaries, and administrative managers.

Advantages of Job Swapping

The organization gets the benefits of two brains instead of one. The organization has a greater source of employees—those who want a permanent part-time job, but will not accept a full-time job. Lateness and absenteeism almost disappear. Boring, routine jobs are more tolerable for short periods of time.

Part-time employees don't get fringe benefits such as sick time, pensions, and sometimes holiday pay. The saving can be

Exhibit 8-2
Job Sharing Worksheet

1. In my organization job sharing could be considered for these jobs: _____
   _____

2. The hours or days of sharing would be: _____

3. The fringe benefits I will have to pay will be: _____
   _____

4. I will (will not) have to get agreement from a union: _____
   _____

5. I expect to have less:
   lateness _____
   absenteeism _____
   time off _____
   sick time _____
   turnover _____
   overtime _____

6. Extra training costs will be $_____

7. More supervision will be needed: Yes _____ No _____

8. There will be communication problems between the job swappers: Yes _____ No _____

9. These problems can be solved by: _____
   _____

These are other considerations pertinent to my organization:

10. _____
    _____

11. _____
    _____

12. _____
    _____

13. I will _____ will not _____ try job sharing.

from 10% to 15% and sometimes up to 30% of payroll costs. Some are paid an hourly rate, so that they don't get paid for time off. Two persons working half-time are more productive than one person working full-time. Job sharers are more energetic and enthusiastic. When one person takes a holiday, the other person can fill in. This way someone is always there to do the job.

If there are layoffs, full-time employees aren't usually affected. If layoffs are necessary for full-time employees, they can be offered a choice: either some employees can be kept full time and the others laid off, or all employees can be kept to share jobs so no one will have to be laid off.

Disadvantages of Job Swapping

One employee may not know what the other is doing. Will one have to correct the other's mistakes? What about unfinished work? What about duplication of work? What about work no one wants to do? Job sharers sometimes have to overlap their times to keep each other informed.

Unions may object to part-time employees who share jobs. Employees and unions may object to job sharing instead of lay-offs. Emphasis is usually placed on seniority.

Extra people may mean additional training costs and supervision. If fringe benefits must be paid, employment costs will increase.

Customers and the public may want to deal with the same employee. But that employee may be absent when needed.

DEHIRING

Dehiring is the opposite of recruiting. Dehiring is getting an employee to terminate employment with an organization. Terminating an employee should only be used as the last disciplinary action. The cost of voluntary turnover is high. Involuntary turnover can also be costly and unpleasant.

If an employee's performance is unsatisfactory, the supervisor or manager should try to get the employee to improve performance. Sometimes a transfer to another job will solve the problem. But, if an employee fails to meet performance standards or correct unacceptable behaviour, that employee should be told what the consequences of those actions will be. The final warning to the employee should be put in writing. Whenever you criticize someone orally or in writing, be certain that you criticize what the person has done (or not done), not who the person is: criticize performance, not personality. When you decide that termination is necessary, the decision should not come as a surprise to the employee.

Tell the employee your decision and provide a choice: quit (resign) or be fired. The first choice will look better on the employee's record. The employee will also save face with fellow employees, family, and friends.

Occasionally, instant dismissal is necessary. For example, the employee may have been involved in major theft, fraud, or physical violence.

Determine in advance what your termination policy will be: how much notification will be given and how much severance compensation will be paid. If you have a union, you will have to follow the terms of the collective agreement. You should also check with the appropriate government authority for legal conditions of dismissal and severance pay.

Effects on Other Employees

Most employees know when an employee has been disciplined. Sometimes it is obvious why an employee has been disciplined. If the reason is not obvious and not personal, the other employees should be told what the reason is. This can be done informally through the grapevine. A public announcement should not be made.

When the employee who is being terminated agrees to quit or resign, you don't have to say anything to the other employees. When an employee is fired, management should tell other employees the reason, unless the reason would be personally damaging to the ex-employee. The reason can be announced formally or informally, depending on the circumstances.

Guidelines for Terminating an Employee

Base the termination on facts. Dismiss the employee as soon as possible after the facts have been established, but preferably dismiss the employee at the end of a day or week.

Tell the employee the reasons for termination. Don't argue: a decision has been made already. Tell the employee of the severance arrangements. Record what happened at the termination meeting, and put this record on the employee's personal file.

COLLECTIVE BARGAINING

All organizations are involved in labour relations. Management may negotiate individually with each employee, collectively with an informal group of employees, collectively through a formal employee committee or association (This Association is sometimes referred to as a company union.), or collectively through a legally certified union.

Why Employees Join a Union

The individual employee feels powerless. By joining together and bargaining collectively, employees hope to bring more effective pressure on management. The employer may be benevolent and the employees may have good pay, benefits, and working conditions, but what has been given voluntarily can be arbitrarily withdrawn. An agreement between management and union would protect the employee's right to receive specified benefits.

Protection against dictatorial and autocratic supervisors and managers is another reason for joining a union. One to one, the employee will usually lose in a management-employee confrontation. Joining a union is one way for employees to retaliate against unpopular management or to ensure fair treatment. Management could arbitrarily treat one employee differently from another with regard to pay, benefits, seniority, grievances, layoff, dismissal, and many other things; under a union contract, the same rules apply to all members of the bargaining unit.

Sometimes employees join unions to find out what's going on. Often the union is the major source of information for employees. Financial and non-financial information about an employer gives employees more bargaining power. Further, the union might help to bring about two-way communications. Employees want to do more than just listen to what management says. They want to have input, especially for the items that will affect them and their jobs. A union offers employees a means of self-expression, for personal development, for recognition, for excitement. Some employees, frustrated by not being promoted, find an outlet for their leadership talents by becoming union stewards and union managers.

Pressure from union leadership convince many people. Some unions actively solicit new members by trying to organize the employees of a company. Many people respond to pressure, especially if the rewards seem great.

Most employees join unions because of the actions or inactions of management. The faults of management in employer-employee relationships result in low morale, decreasing productivity, sabotage, absenteeism, turnover, and collective bargaining. Even organizations with good employer-employee relationships may be unionized because employees might feel powerless since they do not have control over decisions that affect them.

Often a single incident can trigger employee action for collective bargaining: a firing or layoff, a new incentive plan, a new machine, a new policy, a change in ownership.

Management in a small organization may need specialized help in dealing with unions, especially in negotiating the first contract. The advisor, often a lawyer, should be familiar with the terms of the appropriate Labour Relations Act and the practices of the appropriate Labour Relations Board. Management should get a copy of the appropriate Labour Relations Act and other pertinent data from the Ministry or Department of Labour. Typical contents include:

Certification

1. Who can participate in collective bargaining.
2. Who is excluded.
3. How a union acquires bargaining rights.
4. Determining the unit of employees appropriate for collective bargaining.
5. Percentage support needed for certification.
6. Evidence of union membership.
7. Opposition to the union by dissenting employees.
8. Representation votes.

Negotiation

9. After certification, the union gives notice to the employer that it wants to start bargaining.
10. Both parties must meet and bargain in good faith. However, an employer does not have to reveal company data that it wants to keep confidential.
11. Conciliation and other forms of third party intervention to assist the union and employer to reach an agreement.

Contents of Agreements

12. Wages, benefits and working conditions.
13. The agreement must recognize that the union is the exclusive bargaining agent for the employees.
14. The minimum term is one year.
15. There must be no strikes or lockouts during the term of the agreement.
16. Disputes concerning interpretation of the agreement must be resolved by an arbitrator.
17. Union membership and payment of dues may be compulsory as a condition of employment.
18. Procedures for renegotiation or termination of the agreement.

Some employers are opposed to unionization and collective bargaining. Most labour laws prohibit employers from:
1. Interfering with the formation or selection of a union.
2. Promising benefits to employees if they do not join a union.
3. Threatening to close down, move the company's facilities elsewhere, change working conditions, or end certain fringe benefits.
4. Firing or penalizing employees for union activity.
5. Giving financial or other support to a union or a proposed union. The union must be free of any domination by an employer.
6. Preventing employees from discussing unionization.
7. Making coercive speeches to a "captive" audience.

However, the employer may express personal views if the employer does not use threats, coercion, promises, or undue influence. The employer can refer to the company's policies and what the company has done, but cannot make promises or statements concerning the future. The employer should get legal advice before commenting orally or in writing to employees.

For its part, a union is also prohibited from using intimidation to force anyone to join a union—nor can the union interfere with the normal business operations of the employer. An employee may get other employees to sign union cards before work begins or during a work break. But union activity generally is restricted to outside of working hours.

Union organizers who are not employees may not go on the employer's property. The exception is residential property owned by the employer and occupied by employees.

If the employer-employee relationship has been built on co-operation and two-way communication, then the management-union relationship will depend primarily on the employer's attitude. The employer should have a positive attitude and consider the union as a useful medium of communications; the union can have a beneficial influence on employees. The employees will also reflect the attitude of both the employer and the union.

When a formerly friendly and co-operative employer-employee relationship deteriorates, management usually says, "The employees have changed. See what the union has done?" Often the reason is that the employer has changed and the employees are reflecting that change.

Employers should realize that most unions are knowledgeable

and experienced. They are experts in what they do. Collective bargaining is their full-time job.

Exhibit 8-3, "How Unions Work," and Exhibit 8-4 (excerpts from an actual collective agreement between a company and a union) are background information that should help employers have a better understanding of the collective bargaining process.

Exhibit 8-3

How Unions Work

It is at the local level that unions are first organized, and it is there that they perform their most basic function, collective bargaining. Collective bargaining simply means that workers form a group or organization and deal collectively with their employer in discussing and agreeing on wage rates and working conditions.

Before a union can accomplish this there are a number of legal requirements to be met. The vast majority of workers in Canada come under provincial jurisdiction and, while the provisions of the law vary somewhat from province to province, they are in most essentials very similar. A limited number of workers—those engaged in inter-provincial transportation, communication, and a few other industries—are under federal jurisdiction.

The first step in the formation of a union is its organization. The group of workers that the union is to represent must be identified—the plant workers, the office workers, the maintenance workers, people in a particular trade, or a combination of these.

An invitation is extended to the people in the unit asking them to become members of the union. Those who wish to join sign an application form and make an initial payment of dues or an initiation fee to indicate their seriousness. This is usually required by the labour laws.

When the organization has the support of a majority of the people in the unit an application is made to the appropriate Labour Relations Board seeking certification. Certification means that the union is granted official recognition by the government body and is entitled to enter into collective bargaining on behalf of the people in the unit. The law also requires the employer to negotiate with the union and to "bargain in good faith."

The local union thus established would probably be part of a national or international union. Thus, the workers of the Twisty Pretzel Company might form an organization which

cont'd

---

would become Local 123 of the International Pretzel Benders' Union.

The members of the local union elect their own officers—president, vice-president, secretary, treasurer, etc.—who are in charge of the affairs of Local 123. The members pay dues, part of which remains in the local and part going to the international union to pay for the services and assistance it provides to the local.

This service may take various forms. Most national and international unions have a number of specially trained technicians on their staff. These people are able to provide assistance in negotiations with the employers and are usually backed by economists and other research specialists on the union staff. The national or international union may conduct an educational program for all its members. Practically all such unions have regular publications to keep the membership informed on developments of concern to them.

The affairs of the national or international union are governed by periodic conventions, to which each local union is entitled to send delegates. These delegates decide the terms of the union's constitution, the dues that members should be required to pay, and they pass on financial matters.

Once the local union is established, has proven that it has the support of a majority of the workers concerned, and has been officially certified, then the stage is set for collective bargaining to begin.

The most common procedure is for the members of the local union to hold a meeting, or more often a series of meetings, to decide on proposals which will be made to management. They also select some of their members to act on the bargaining committee. They may decide to ask the union to which they are affiliated to provide the assistance of an experienced negotiator, or a specialist on such technical subjects as pensions.

The contract proposals advanced by the union may cover a wide variety of subjects. Such matters as wages and hours are, of course, the most common, but they are by no means the only ones. Suggestions may be advanced with regard to vacations, statutory holidays (observance of Boxing Day, etc.), a pension plan, medical insurance, seniority provisions governing promotions, and a grievance procedure. The members of the local vote on exactly what proposals are to be made. The bargaining committee they have elected then arranges to meet the representatives of management. The spokesmen for man-

cont'd

agement may be the head of the company, the director of the personnel department, or other company officials, depending, as a rule, on the size of the company.

Bargaining is often a slow process. The proposals advanced by the union may be met by counter-proposals by the company and there is a period of discussion and often concessions by each side. Periodically the two groups engaged in bargaining report back to their superiors; in the case of the union this means that the bargaining committee reports to a membership meeting where it may receive additional instructions.

In the vast majority of cases voluntary agreement is finally reached between management and the workers. The terms of the agreement are then written into a contract and this governs the wages, hours and other conditions of employment in that particular company for a specified period—normally one, two or three years.

If the two parties find it impossible to reach agreement then methods are provided in the labour laws of the various provinces, and in federal legislation, for government assistance. The form this takes varies somewhat in the various provinces.

In many instances the first stage is the appointment of a conciliation officer. This is an official of the government's labour department. He meets with the union and with management to explore the nature and extent of their differences. He may also bring the two groups together in an effort to have them agree. If he succeeds then a contract is signed. If he fails the discussions move on to the next step.

This is most frequently the establishment of a Conciliation Board which is normally composed of three people—one nominated by the company, one by the union, and the third, the chairman, selected by the other two members. If they cannot agree on a chairman, he may be appointed by the Minister of Labour.

The Board conducts hearings and listens to the arguments of both sides and then makes a report. The findings of the board are not binding on either party; they are intended rather to influence a voluntary agreement. If such an agreement is reached a contract is signed and the matter ends there. If there is no agreement, the workers, after a period specified in the labour law, are free to go on strike.

The decision as to whether they will strike rests, of course, with the workers concerned, and they vote on what action should be taken. While strikes naturally attract a good deal of public attention the fact is that in about 97 per cent of the

cont'd

cases agreement is reached and a contract signed without any strike action.

Once the contract is in effect, one of the most important sections is that concerning a method for the settlement of grievances. The contract is intended to provide an orderly plan for dealing with most employee-employer relationships, and this is particularly true as far as grievances are concerned.

The worker's grievance may have to do with any one of a great number of matters. He may feel that he is not receiving the proper rate of pay for the specific job he is working on; that he is not being allowed the vacation that he is entitled to; that he was not paid for overtime he had worked; or that there is something wrong with the conditions under which he has to do his job. If he has a complaint he has the right to file a grievance.

The contract sets forth the course to be followed in processing the grievance. As a rule, at the first stage, an effort is made to settle it in the department where the worker is employed. In this step the key people may be the foreman of the department and the union shop steward. The shop steward is one of the workers who has been chosen by his fellow-employees, through the union, to represent the interests of those who work in his section.

If a settlement is not reached there, then the matter is taken to a higher level; and so on up through the ranks of management and involving more senior union officers or officials. If, after this process has been exhausted, no agreement is reached, then the whole matter is usually placed before an outside third party, called an arbitrator, or before several people on an arbitration commission, and the decision then given is binding on the company, the employee and the union representing him.

Another matter that is likely to be dealt with in the contract is the collection of union dues by means of a check-off. This means that the employer deducts union dues from the employees' pay—just as income tax, unemployment insurance contributions and donations to various charitable causes are deducted.

Whether or not all employees are required to join the union depends on the terms agreed upon between the workers and the employer. If there is a closed shop then the employer agrees to hire only workers who are already members of the union. A more common provision is what is known as the union shop. This means that workers, usually after an initial proba-

cont'd

tionary period, usually 30 days, are required to join the union. A modification of this is called the Rand Formula or Agency Shop. This means that employees are not required to actually join the union but they are required to pay union dues. This plan is based on the philosophy that all employees benefit from the activities of the union and should, therefore, contribute to its maintenance. It should be remembered with reference to all these plans that the union is required to obtain and prove the support of a majority of the workers before it can attain a position to gain such provisions.

Source: Public Relations Department of the Canadian Labour Congress, Ottawa. Reprinted by permission of the Canadian Labour Congress.

Exhibit 8-4
Collective Agreement (excerpts)

Agreement effective as of the 1st day of January, 19–, between the A.B.C. Company (hereinafter called "The Company") and the XYZ Union (hereinafter called "The Union").

INDEX
Article

General Purpose
1. Recognition and Scope
2. Relationship
3. Management Rights
4. Reporting for Work
5. Working Conditions
6. Hours of Work and Overtime
7. Specified Holidays
8. Vacations with Pay
9. Wages
10. Shift Bonus
12. Employee Displacements Through Technological Change
13. Seniority
14. Probationary Employees
16. Discharge and Suspension Grievances
17. Stewards
18. Grievances
19. Arbitration
22. Check-Off
23. Representatives
24. Information to the Union

cont'd

General Purpose

The general purpose of this Agreement between the Company and the Union is to establish and maintain:

a. Orderly collective bargaining relations;
b. a procedure for the prompt and equitable handling of grievances;
c. satisfactory working conditions, hours and wages; for all employees who are subject to the provisions of this Agreement.

ARTICLE 1
Recognition and Scope

1.01 The Company recognizes that the Union is the Collective Bargaining Agent for all of its employees employed on jobs which are at present hourly rated jobs except the office, technical and personnel staff, watchmen, timekeepers, time study personnel, clerical employees and foremen. It is provided in this connection that no job which is presently hourly rated shall be during the term of this Agreement removed from the bargaining unit.

1.03 The Union agrees that, in recognition of the fact that efficient and economic production is in the interest of both parties, it will promote amongst its members good workmanship and regular attendance. It is further agreed by the Union that the employees will at all times protect the property of the Company against damage by themselves or others.

ARTICLE 2
Relationship

2.01 a. The Company shall not discriminate against any employee because of such employee's membership in the Union, or his Union activities within the scope of this Agreement.

b. The Union, or its officers, members or agents shall not intimidate or coerce any employee or employees into membership in the Union.

cont'd

2.02 During the term of this Agreement the Company agrees that there shall be no lock-out and the Union agrees that there shall be no slowdown, strike or other work stoppage or interference with work.

2.03 The Union agrees that unless duly authorized:
   a. Union meetings will not be held on Company premises.
   b. No employee or Union official will solicit membership in the Union, collect dues, or engage in any Union activity on Company time, during his working hours, or the working hours of any employee, except as provided for in this Agreement.

Violation by an employee of any of the foregoing provisions shall be cause for discharge or for discipline of such employees by the Company, but such actions are to be subject to the provisions of Article 18.

ARTICLE 3
Management Rights

3.01 It is recognized that management of the plant and direction of the working forces are fixed exclusively in the Company, which maintains all rights and responsibilities of management not specifically modified by this Agreement.

The exercise of such rights shall include but not be limited to:
   a. The right to hire, assign, increase and/or decrease the working forces, promote, demote, transfer and make temporary lay-offs for lack of business and materials.
   b. The determination of: The number and location of plants, the product to be manufactured, the methods of manufacturing, schedules of production, kinds and locations of machines and tools to be used, processes of manufacturing and assembling, the engineering and design of its products, and the control of materials and parts to be incorporated in the products produced.
   c. The making and enforcement of rules and regulations, not inconsistent with this Agreement, relating to discipline, safety, and general conduct of the employees, and to suspend or discharge or otherwise discipline employees for just cause.

3.02 Claims of discriminatory upgrading, demotion or trans-

cont'd

fer, or a claim that an employee has been suspended or discharged without just cause may be made the subject of a grievance and dealt with as provided in this Agreement.

3.03 To enable the Company to keep its products abreast of scientific advancements the Company may from time to time, without reference to seniority hereinafter set forth, hire, teach, transfer or assign duties to technically trained men and technical students and deal with them as it deems advisable. This practice, however, shall not adversely affect the employees in the bargaining unit.

3.04 The Company agrees that these functions will be exercised in a manner not inconsistent with the terms of this Agreement.

ARTICLE 4
Reporting for Work

4.01 When an employee reports for work at the normal starting time of the shift and his regular job is not available, he will receive alternate work or pay equivalent to four hours at his hourly wage rate. This will not apply under the following conditions:

  a. Where the employee has been informed a minimum of six hours in advance of his regular starting time that he is not to report for work.
  b. Where the plant or part of it or its equipment, is damaged by fire, lightning, flood or tempest.
  c. Where interruption of work is due to circumstances beyond the Company's reasonable control.
  d. Where the employee is not willing to accept alternate work. Such alternate work must not be of an unreasonable nature by way of safety, dress requirements, physical demands, etc.
  e. When the employee fails to keep the Company informed of his latest address and telephone number, the Company shall be relieved of its responsibility with regard to notice not to report for work. The Company will supply an authorized "Change of Address" card for this purpose, which will be available upon request at the Employment Offices.

4.02 When an employee reports for work at the normal starting time of the shift and his regular job is not available for the full four hours:

cont'd

a. If no further work is available he will then be paid at his hourly wage rate for the balance of the four hours not worked.

b. If alternate work is available then the employee will be assigned to that work and he will receive a minimum of pay equivalent to four hours at his hourly wage rate for the shift.

4.03 An employee is expected to give prior notice when reporting for work following an illness. However, in the event such notice is not given and such absence exceeds one working day, he shall not qualify for work or pay pursuant to Sections 4.01 and 4.02 unless he has informed the Company by no later than 12:00 noon on his normally scheduled work day immediately prior to the day that he will be returning to work.

4.04 Employees who are called in outside of their regularly assigned hours will receive not less than three hours' work or pay at the appropriate premium rate provided under Section 6.03 b. This shall not apply if such is immediately prior to or succeeding his regular shift, or if a break is requested by the employee. In such cases, Article 6 will apply.

ARTICLE 5
Working Conditions

5.01 The Company shall continue to make reasonable provision for the safety and health of its employees at the factories during the hours of their employment. The Union will co-operate with the Company in maintaining good working conditions and will assist in assuring observance of safety rules.

5.02 The Company welcomes from the Union, its members, or any employee, suggestions regarding safety and health.

ARTICLE 6
Hours of Work and Overtime

6.01 The normal hours of work shall be 40 hours per week consisting of five eight-hour days, Monday to Friday inclusive. This is not to be read or construed as a guarantee to provide work for any period whatsoever.

6.02 Hours of work in excess of 8 hours per day, Monday to Friday, inclusive, and hours of work on Saturday

cont'd

and Sunday, will be treated as overtime hours and will be paid for at a premium rate as provided under Section 6.03 b. below, except that when employees change shifts at their own request, they shall not be entitled to such premium rate by reason of the fact that they have worked two eight-hour shifts in the 24-hour period.

6.03 a. In computing daily overtime hours, a day shall be the twenty-four hour period following the regular starting time of the shift on which the employee is working except that the provisions of this Article shall not apply so that hours paid at a premium rate for work performed on an employee's second day following his regular work week entitle him to a premium rate for any hours worked as part of his normal hours of work.

b. Overtime hours worked will be paid for at a premium rate calculated on the basis of one and one-half times an employee's hourly wage rate except in the case of Sunday, when that day is the second day following an employee's normal work week (that is, Monday to Friday inclusive), in which case the overtime hours worked will be paid for at a premium rate calculated on the basis of two times an employee's hourly wage rate.

6.04 For the purposes of calculating payment for time worked under this Article 6 and under Article 7, time worked on a scheduled shift commencing prior to 10:00 p.m. shall be treated as if worked on the calendar day on which such shift commenced. Time worked on a scheduled shift commencing at or after 10:00 p.m. shall be treated as work performed on the immediately following calendar day.

6.05 As far as possible, overtime hours worked will be equally distributed amongst the employees. Each employee is expected to co-operate with the Company in the performance of such work and the Company agrees to accept reasonable grounds for the employee declining to perform such work.

6.06 The Company may change work schedules, including the scheduling of more or less than the normal working time, but will confer with representatives of the local Union before making any general change in group, department or plant work schedules.

cont'd

6.07 In no case will an overtime premium rate be paid twice for the same hours worked.

ARTICLE 7
Specified Holidays

7.01 The Company agrees to pay an employee, as provided under Section 7.04 below, for the following specified holidays without requiring an employee to render service:

New Year's Day
Good Friday
Victoria Day (Empire Day)
Dominion Day
Civic Holiday
Labour Day
Thanksgiving Day
Christmas Day

7.02 a. For the application of the Sections of this Article, a specified holiday as listed above shall be observed on the day on which it occurs, except that if such a holiday occurs on a Saturday it shall be observed on the preceding Friday and except, also, if such a holiday occurs on a Sunday it shall be observed on the following Monday.

7.04 The specified holiday pay as referred to in this Article will be calculated on the basis of the employee's hourly wage rate multiplied by the number of hours in the employee's standard work day or half shift as applicable.

7.06 An employee required to work on the day on which the specified holiday is observed, will receive overtime pay as shown in Article 6, in addition to the specified holiday pay.

7.07 If the specified holiday is observed during an employee's annual vacation, payment for such holiday will be made. Annual vacation, or specified holidays in a pay period, shall be considered worked time for the purpose of qualifying for specified holiday pay.

ARTICLE 8
Vacations with Pay

8.01 Annual vacations will be paid on the following basis:
   i) Six weeks after 30 years' continuous service if completed by December 31st.

cont'd

ii) Five weeks after 25 years' continuous service if completed by December 31st.

iii) Four weeks after 15 years' continuous service if completed by December 31st.

iv) Three weeks after 5 years' continuous service if completed by December 31st.

v) Two weeks after 1 years' continuous service if completed by July 31st.

8.02 Vacations will be scheduled by the Company and shall be completed within the calendar year. It is not permissible to postpone the vacation period or any part thereof from one year to another. The Company may in respect of a fifth and sixth week of vacation as set out in Section 8.01 above, exercise an option to make payment for such week in accordance with Section 8.04, in lieu of scheduling vacation time.

8.04 The allowance for each week of vacation will be determined by multiplying the employee's hourly wage rate by the number of hours in the employee's regular weekly schedule. This will not include hours for which overtime premium is paid.

8.05 a. An employee with less than 12 months' continuous service will be paid a vacation allowance calculated on the basis of four percent of the employee's earnings during the period from the employee's date of hiring to July 31.

b. An employee who has been laid off, or an employee who has had leave under the provisions of Section 15.03 b. for a period in excess of 60 working days during the vacation year (August 1st to July 31st) will be paid vacation pay to an amount of 4%, 6%, 8%, 10%, or 12%, whichever figure is applicable, of his gross earnings during the year.

8.06 a. An employee with less than 12 months' continuous service with the Company, whose service is discontinued, will be paid four percent of the employee's earnings.

b. An employee with more than 12 months' continuous service with the Company, whose service is discontinued, will be paid two percent for each week of vacation entitlement.

cont'd

ARTICLE 9
Wages

9.01 All job classifications covered by this Agreement shall be paid on the basis of hourly wage rates. The established job classifications, their titles, code numbers, Labour Grade and hourly wage rates of pay shall be contained in the Hourly Wage Rates and Classification Book, which shall be known herein as "The Rate Book" and which shall form part of this Agreement.

9.02 The Rate Book shall contain an hourly wage rate for each job classification to be known as the Job Rate. The Job Rate shall be the rate for the Labour Grade in which the job classification has been ranked by evaluation.

9.03 The Labour Grades and respective Job Rates in effect during the term of this Agreement shall be as set forth in Schedule ≠1 and ≠2 of Appendix "A" hereto.

9.04 The responsibility for evaluation of any work shall continue to be vested in the Company. Evaluation will continue to be made on the basis of the Job Evaluation Programme (including the Job Rating Plan for Hourly Paid Classifications). The Job Evaluation Programme as such, having been selected by the Company, may not form the subject of a grievance. When new and/or changed job classifications are implemented by the Company, the Union will be notified of the resulting amendments to the Rate Book, together with the date of implementation, the department(s) and employee(s) affected.

9.10 TRANSFER AND RECALL WAGE RATE
DETERMINATION

For the purpose of this Section, a transfer is defined as the assignment of an employee from one job classification to another, as contained in the Rate Book, and which is accompanied by a change in the Company's records; or as the assignment of an employee to another job classification which extends for three weeks or more. An employee's hourly rate when transferred shall be determined in accordance with the appropriate section below.

  a. An employee who is transferred by reason of Article 13 of the Collective Agreement (Seniority) or for reason of health or safety will be paid his pre-transfer

cont'd

hourly wage rate for the balance of the pay period in which the transfer is made and thereafter shall,

i) if transferred to a job classification ranked in the same or a lower Labour Grade and his pre-transfer rate is the Job Rate, he shall be paid the Job Rate for the job classification to which he is transferred.

ii) if transferred to a job classification ranked in the same or a lower Labour Grade, and his pre-transfer rate is a step rate, he shall be paid as follows:

1) if his pre-transfer rate is equal to or greater than the Job Rate for the job classification to which he is transferred he shall be paid the Job Rate for such job classification.

2) if his pre-transfer rate is less than the Job Rate for the job classification to which he is transferred, he shall be paid his pre-transfer rate and complete the balance of the time periods required to qualify for the Job Rate of the job classification to which he is transferred.

iii) if transferred to a job classification ranked in a higher Labour Grade, the employee will be paid as follows:

1) if his pre-transfer rate is the Job Rate he will be paid one step rate below the Job Rate for the job classification to which he is transferred and complete the necessary time period to qualify for the Job Rate.

2) if his pre-transfer rate is a step rate, he shall be paid at the same rate, or the start rate for the job classification to which he is transferred, whichever is the higher, and complete the time periods necessary to qualify for the Job Rate.

b. An employee who is transferred at the request of the Company for utilization of his applicable skills, when there is work for him on his regular job, and not as a result of other causes set forth herein, shall be paid his pre-transfer hourly wage rate or the Job Rate for the job classification to which he is transferred, whichever is the higher, for the duration of such transfer. Such hourly wage rate shall be effective from the date of transfer.

cont'd

c. An employee who is transferred at his own request shall be paid in the manner outlined in Section a., i), ii) or iii) hereof, except that the hourly wage rate to be paid in the job classification to which he is transferred shall become effective on the date of such transfer.

d. An employee who is transferred because of inability, inefficiency or demotion for cause, shall be paid at a relative position in the progression schedule applicable to the job classification to which he is transferred. Such hourly wage rate shall be effective from the date of transfer.

ARTICLE 10
Shift Bonus

10.01 Employees required to work on any shift starting before 6:00 a.m. or after 12 noon, will be paid a shift bonus of 20 cents per hour.

10.02 On three shift operations there shall be 8 hours in-plant time. There shall be no assigned lunch period for employees on operations of an uninterruptable nature. Employees on three shifts interruptable operations, for which lunch period has been assigned, will be paid an allowance of .4 hours at their hourly rate.

ARTICLE 12
Employee Displacements Through
Technological Change

12.01 This Article shall have application when the Company introduces new technology in the form of capital equipment, and such introduction has the initial result of:
i) displacing an employee, or
ii) changing the immediate job of an employee by establishing a different labour grade.
Where five (5) or more employees are affected as set out in either i) or ii) above, the Company will notify the Union as far in advance as practicable and, upon request, the Company will arrange a meeting with the Union for the purpose of discussing the effects on the employment status of such employees in applying this Article.

12.02 The Company will provide a training period of up to fifteen (15) working days (which may be extended by agreement) on a new or changed job created as a

cont'd

result of the introduction of new capital equipment under Section 12.01 to an employee with seniority who is thereby displaced, provided that the number of training periods afforded hereunder will not exceed the number of such new or changed jobs. An employee will be selected for a training period on the basis of seniority provided the Company has reasonable evidence in its records or as furnished by the employee or the Union that the employee has transferable skills which would enable him to meet the normal requirements of the job within a maximum period of fifteen (15) working days. If the new or changed job thus created is classified in an occupational classification with a lower labour grade than the classification to which the employee was assigned before the new equipment was introduced, the employee may elect to be placed in accordance with Section 13.07 g.

An employee will be permitted not more than one opportunity for training under this Section, it being understood that the Company shall be required under these provisions to grant only one period of training under the application of this Section on a new or changed job. A displaced employee unable to qualify for a training period as provided herein will be subject to the provisions of Section 13.07 g. in locating another job. Further, an employee selected for training hereunder but unable to meet the normal requirements of the work of such job during the maximum period of fifteen (15) working days will be subject to the provisions of Section 13.07 g. in locating another job.

ARTICLE 13
Seniority

13.01 The seniority of each employee covered by this Agreement shall be established after a period of probation of sixty worked days and shall then count from the date of employment with the Company, except in the case of students hired during the school vacation, in which case seniority shall be established after a period of probation of ninety (90) worked days.

13.02 a. An employee's seniority date (departmental, intra-plant, or inter-plant) shall be his last hiring date, except that upon returning to work following a lay-off or illness in excess of 12 months, his seniority date

cont'd

shall be adjusted in accordance with his length of service pursuant to the provisions of Section 13.09 hereof. An employee shall acquire departmental, intra-plant, and inter-plant seniority on the following basis:

    i) On completion of sixty worked days with the Company an employee shall acquire departmental seniority.

    ii) On completion of ten months' service with the Company, an employee shall acquire intra-plant seniority.

    iii) On completion of sixty months' service with the Company, an employee shall acquire inter-plant seniority.

b. For purposes of lay-off (meaning here and elsewhere in this Article lay-off from employment) or transfers due to lack of work, an employee shall exercise his seniority as follows:

    i) An employee with not more than 10 months' seniority shall be limited to exercising his departmental seniority.

    ii) An employee with more than 10 months' seniority but not more than 60 months' seniority will first exercise his departmental seniority and then shall be limited to exercising his intra-plant seniority.

    iii) An employee with seniority in excess of 60 months will first exercise his departmental seniority and then shall exercise his inter-plant seniority.

c. In the event an employee with seniority, as defined in this Section, is laid off, he will be included in the inter-plant recall list.

13.04 There shall be no lay-off of personnel within a department or plant until probationary employees of such department or plant have been laid off.

13.05 As applied to individual employee(s), the Company may lay off an employee up to a total of 15 working days in each calendar year without regard to the seniority provisions of this Agreement. Time lost for the following causes will not be subject to the seniority provisions of the Agreement. Neither will it be counted in the 15-day exception referred to herein:

a. Time lost by an employee during the annual vacation shutdown for his Division as a result of such em-

cont'd

ployee's vacation entitlement being less than the shutdown period. It being understood that for the purposes of this sub-section a. such time so lost will not exceed 3 calendar weeks.

b. If vacation shutdowns are scheduled at varying times in various Departments, Divisions or Plants, in no case shall an individual employee who was employed in an area that was shut down for vacation purposes and was affected by sub-section a., subsequently be affected again by the provisions of subsection a., if during the same calendar year, he is employed in another area. The Company will not transfer an employee for the purpose of exposing him to the provisions of 13.05 a. more than once in a calendar year.

c. Time lost by an employee during days on which annual inventory is taken, up to a maximum of two days.

d. Time lost by an employee due expressly to a shutdown caused by fire, lightning, flood or tempest, causing damage to the plant, or part of it, or its equipment.

13.06 a. The Company will maintain seniority boards in each department showing the departmental seniority of each employee in that department.

b. Copies of the inter-plant seniority lists shall be supplied to the Union every six months. The Company will continue to post copies of such lists in appropriate locations.

c. The Company will supply the Union with the following information:
   i) Starts, quits, discharges, transfers and lay-offs of employees other than lay-offs under Section 13.05 above. Such information will be supplied on a pay period basis.
   ii) A copy of notices of recall as referred to in Section 13.07 d. below.

d. Upon reasonable request to the foreman, the departmental steward shall have the opportunity to scrutinize the departmental recall list maintained by the foreman.

13.07 Lay-offs or transfers due to lack of work will be governed by the following provisions:

cont'd

a. Seniority as defined in Sections 13.02 and 13.03 hereof.
b. Seniority will be the major factor governing lay-offs or transfers due to lack of work, in accordance with Section 13.07 g. i) and ii) hereof, subject to the retained employees being able to meet the normal requirements of the work.
c. The Company will give seven calendar days' notice in writing to an employee of a lay-off, the duration of which is expected to exceed fifteen calendar days. Such notice will indicate, whenever reasonably possible, whether the lay-off is expected to be of short or indefinite duration. This provision will not, however, apply with respect to the following:
  i) Probationary employees;
  ii) Lay-offs under Section 13.05 although the employee will be informed when the lay-off takes place thereunder;
  iii) Lay-offs resulting from lack of work owing to any slow-down, strike, or other work stoppage or interference with work by employees covered by this Agreement;
  iv) Lay-offs resulting from such matters as fire, lightning, flood, tempest or power failure.
d. Employees who are laid off shall be recalled in order of their seniority provided they are able to meet the normal requirements of the job. The Company will confirm an employee's recall by registered letter sent to the employee's last address on record with the Company as furnished by the employee. An employee upon being recalled shall notify the Company within three (3) working days of receiving such letter of his intention to return to work and shall return to work no later than ten (10) working days from the day such letter is mailed except in the case of verified illness.
e. An employee who has been transferred within his department, as a result of the provisions of this Article, shall be given an opportunity of returning to his original job.
f. An employee who has been transferred to another department, as a result of the provisions of this Article, shall be given an opportunity, if and when production conditions improve, and before additional

cont'd

employees are hired in the department, of returning to his original job.

    i) The provisions of e. and f. will be limited to a period of two years from the date of original transfer. An employee who declines the opportunity of return under e. and f. hereto shall forfeit the right to return thereafter.

    ii) An employee who exhausts his rights of return under the provisions of Section 13.07 f. i), and an employee who has lost his right of return because of lay-off, may apply in writing to the appropriate Employment Office for a one-year extension of such rights, and such request will be granted by the Company, provided the employee, at the time any return is effected has the skill and ability to meet the normal requirements of the job within a maximum period of five working days of re-familiarization.

    The employee may re-apply in writing for maintenance of such return rights for an additional year after each one year extension and such application will be accepted by the Company subject to the aforesaid conditions. Applications hereunder shall be made during the two-week period immediately prior to the expiration of any annual extension.

g. i) The Company and the Union recognize that it is desirable to keep displacement of one employee by another (bumping) to a minimum, consistent with employees maintaining their seniority rights. Therefore, in locating a job, in accordance with Section 13.07 g. ii) hereof, which is one held by an employee with less seniority or an open job, the procedure will be to commence from the bottom of the appropriate seniority list and work upwards.

    ii) The procedure for the purpose of locating another job for which an employee may be eligible, will be applied by the Company in relation to the job from which he is about to be transferred, provided he has the skill and ability to perform the job as verified by Company records, or as furnished by the employee or the Union.

13.08 An employee shall maintain and accumulate seniority under the following conditions:

cont'd

a. During absence due to illness, not to exceed fifty-two consecutive weeks.

b. During leave of absence granted by the Company in writing.

c. During a lay-off not to exceed 12 consecutive months.

13.10 An employee shall lose his seniority standing under the following conditions:

a. If the employee leaves the employ of the Company.

b. If continuously laid off for more than thirty-six months.

c. If discharged for just cause and such discharge is not reversed through the grievance procedure provided herein.

d. If an employee fails to report for work in accordance with the provisions of Section 13.07 d.

e. If an employee overstays a leave of absence for a period of seven working days without the written permission of the Company.

13.11 An employee of the Company shall, upon being transferred to a job within the bargaining unit, have seniority computed from the last date of hiring, if he has previously completed a period of sixty worked days as an hourly-rated employee.

13.12 A department steward who has five or more years' seniority shall have preferential seniority, exercisable within his department in respect of a lay-off or transfer out of the department resulting from lack of work, provided he can meet the normal requirements of the work available. Chief Stewards shall have preferential seniority on the same basis in their respective Zones.

13.15 An employee with seniority who has been absent from work due to illness or accident and, when medically cleared to return to work, is unable in the opinion of the Company to perform the normal requirements of the work of the job performed by him immediately prior to such illness or accident, will be eligible for an open job, provided he has the skill and ability to meet the normal requirements of the work.

ARTICLE 14
Probationary Employees

14.01 Where a probationary employee is transferred to another department he will be required to complete 60 worked

cont'd

days (90 worked days in the case of students as referred to in Section 13.01) from the date of initial transfer before acquiring seniority. On completion of this 60 worked days (90 worked days in the case of students as referred to in Section 13.01), the seniority of the employee will be counted from the hiring date in the original department.

14.02 The Company has full right to discharge probationary employees if, in the opinion of the Company, they do not meet the standard required of them by the Company. A grievance may be filed by a probationary employee who has been discharged, and who alleges that such discharge is an act of discrimination by the Company for reason of the employee's Union activities.

ARTICLE 15
Leave of Absence

15.01 Leave of absence without pay will be granted to:
   a. two members of the Union with seniority standing for full time Local 504, Union work, and
   b. three members of the Union with seniority standing for full time National Union work,
   for the duration of this Agreement or until the completion of his mission, whichever first occurs. Upon completion of his mission or upon the expiration of this Agreement, whichever first occurs, he will be given re-employment on the basis of his continuity of seniority in his former position or in a similar position at the rate prevailing at the time of such re-employment. An employee who is granted such leave of absence under this Section and who returns to work on completion of his mission will be ineligible for another such leave within a period of three months. Continuity of seniority will only be granted to such member upon the resumption of employment with the Company.

15.02 Upon written request by the Union and if reasonable notice is given, the Company will grant leave of absence to employee(s) without pay for Union business.
   During leave of absence under this Section the employee will maintain and accumulate seniority.
   Under this Section except for leaves of absence due to grievance and arbitration participation and negotiation preparations and processes, not more than three hundred (300) man-days total leave of absence will be

cont'd

granted in any one calendar year.

It is understood that the Company may withhold leaves requested by the Union and ask the Union to substitute other employees if the numbers of leaves requested in respect of any job, department or division interferes with the operating requirements of the Company.

15.03 a. Subject to the following conditions the Company will grant leave of absence without pay to a pregnant employee at her request:

i) Such employee must have one year's seniority.

ii) The Company may require medical verification of the employee's condition.

iii) Leave will normally be granted for a period of three months prior to confinement and two months following confinement.

Nothing in this Section shall restrict the Company from requiring a pregnant employee prior to her confinement to go on such leave of absence or for such longer period as the Company decides on the grounds that her physical condition while at work constitutes a hazard to herself, her fellow employees, or is interfering with her ability to perform her work.

b. The Company will not unreasonably withhold leave of absence without pay when requested by employees for other personal reasons.

ARTICLE 16
Discharge and Suspension Grievances

16.01 A claim by an employee that he has been suspended or discharged without just cause from his employment may be treated as a grievance and a written statement of such grievance, signed by the employee, must be lodged by the Union or the employee with the Union Relations Department of the Company within four working days immediately following the date of suspension or discharge, and the case shall be disposed of within ten working days in the case of a suspension and within six working days in the case of a discharge after the date of filing of the grievance, except where such case goes to arbitration.

Except where more than two employees from the same Department are suspended or discharged, the employee, if he so requests, shall have the right to see his Steward prior to leaving the plant, at a time and place designated

cont'd

by the Company.

The four working day limitation referred to above will not apply if the suspended or discharged employee is able to prove his inability to communicate with the Company by reason of illness.

16.02 Such suspension or discharge grievance may be settled:
   a. By confirming the Management's action in suspending or dismissing the employee, or
   b. By reinstating the employee with full compensation for time lost, or
   c. By any other arrangement which is just and equitable in the opinion of the parties or a Board of Arbitration.

ARTICLE 17
Stewards

17.01 Definitions:
   a. "Departmental Steward" is a person elected or appointed by the Union members of his department to represent the department in which he is employed.
   b. "Chief Steward" is a person elected or appointed by the Union members of his zone as their representative.

17.02 The Company acknowledges the right of the Union to elect or appoint one steward for each foreman or each department, whichever is the greater in number, to assist employees in the presentation of their grievances.

17.03 The Union acknowledges that stewards as well as other members of the Union committees, and the Union officers, will continue to perform their regular duties on behalf of the Company, and that:
   a. Such persons will not leave their regular duties without obtaining permission from their foreman or immediate supervisor who will be given a reasonable explanation for the requested absence.
   b. When resuming their regular duties after engaging in duties on behalf of the Union they will report to their foreman or supervisor immediately upon their return.
   c. Any Union representative who is privileged by this Agreement to take up Union business in a department other than his own will also report to the foreman of that department at the time.

17.04 A steward will assist in the grievance procedure as set forth in Article 18 except that in the absence of a steward the Chief Steward may act in his place.

cont'd

17.05 A departmental steward deputized by the Union to substitute for a Chief Steward may carry out the Chief Steward's duties on behalf of the Union in the event of the Chief Steward's authorized absence from the plant.

17.06 The Company will pay for time lost while on Company premises and authorized to be absent from regular duties under Section 17.03 during his normal hours of work as set out in Article 6, as follows:

    a. 50% of time lost to a maximum of 1½ hours' pay in any one week to Department Stewards.

    b. 50% of time lost to a maximum of 2½ hours' pay in any one week to Job Evaluation Panel members.

    c. 50% of time lost to a maximum of 5½ hours' pay in any one week to Chief Stewards.

    d. 50% of time lost by Grievance Panel to a maximum of 2½ hours' pay in any one week.

    e. The Company will supply to the Union a list showing the number of hours paid to each of the Stewards or Committee members named above.

17.07 If requested by the employee concerned, a copy of a written notice of discipline will be given to the employee's departmental Steward for the information of the Union as soon as practicable.

17.08 Time lost by a Chief Steward or a Steward during his normal hours of work as set out in Article 6, while on Company premises and when authorized to be absent from his regular duties under Section 17.03, shall not thereby disqualify him for premium rate under Article 6 to which he would otherwise be entitled.

ARTICLE 18
Grievances

18.01 Nothing herein shall prevent an individual employee from discussing a complaint with his Foreman, or submitting a grievance on his own behalf as provided herein, except that if the Union has taken up a grievance on behalf of the employee with his consent, the withdrawal of such consent shall not prevent the Union from processing the grievance under the grievance provisions hereof.

18.02 First Stage: The employee may request permission of his Foreman to discuss and/or prepare a grievance with his

cont'd

Department Steward as provided in Section 18.07. A written grievance, signed by the employee or a representative number of the employees concerned, shall be submitted by the Steward and/or the employee to the Foreman concerned. The Foreman will sign the grievance and indicate the time and date received. The Foreman shall give his answer in writing to the Department Steward within four working days of the date on which he receives the grievance. The Foreman will, on the same day, give a copy of his answer to the employee(s) and he will also arrange for two additional copies to be given to the Zone Chief Steward.

18.03 Second Stage: If a settlement is not reached under the first stage above, the grievance shall be submitted to the Foreman's immediate supervisor by the Zone Chief Steward within thirty calendar days from the date of the Foreman's answer under Section 18.02. The supervisor shall sign and date the grievance. The grievance will be referred by the Foreman's immediate supervisor to the Union Relations Department of the Company.
However, within five working days from the date of the Foreman's answer under Section 18.02, a meeting may be held between the Zone Chief Steward and such supervisor to discuss the grievance, if requested by either the Zone Chief Steward or such supervisor.

18.04 The Union Relations Department will arrange a meeting within two weeks of the date on which the grievance was submitted to the Zone Chief Steward. The Manager of Union Relations, or his appointee, shall give an answer in writing within ten working days of such meeting. Meetings with the Union Relations Department in connection with 13.13, however, shall take place within two weeks of the date of receipt of the grievance.

18.05 During the Second Stage meeting as provided above, the Union, or the employee, may be represented by a representative of the National Office of the Union, one full-time official of the Local Union, a maximum of three members of the Union Grievance Panel who shall be employees of the Company and any employee possessed of factual knowledge touching on the matter in question. The Company shall also have the right to have present any officers, officials or agents of the Company.

18.06 The time limits set out in Section 18.02, 18.03 and

cont'd

18.04, shall be strictly observed. Any grievance not filed within the time limits established by the provisions of this Agreement shall be considered disposed of or settled. If the Company fails to comply with the time limits established by the provisions of this Agreement the Union may file the grievance in the next succeeding stage. It is expressly provided, however, that the parties may agree in writing in respect to any grievance to extend and/or waive any of the time limits imposed on either of them.

18.07 The designation of the time and place involved in the discussions and meetings and/or for the preparation of written grievances as provided in the foregoing sections of this Article shall be subject to the direction of the foreman or supervisor concerned and shall be held during working hours on the day of the request or as soon as practical thereafter.

18.08 The Company shall not be liable for retroactive payments prior to six months from the date of filing of a grievance hereunder. It is understood that a grievance should be filed within twelve months of the date of the occurrence which gave rise to it. In the event, however, a grievance is filed more than twelve months after the date of the occurrence which gave rise to it, the Company's liability for retroactive payment shall be reduced by the number of days that the period from the date of such occurrence, to the date of the filing of the grievance, is greater than twelve months.

18.09 It is understood that the Company may bring forward and give to the Union at any time any grievance:
  a. With respect to the conduct of the Union, its officers or committeemen.
  b. With respect to the conduct of the employees generally.
  c. With respect to the application or interpretation of any provision of this Agreement.
The grievance shall first be presented in writing to the officials of the Union and a meeting will be held within seven calendar days with the Union and its representatives. Failure to agree within a period of four calendar days subsequent to the meeting will permit the Company to refer the matter to a Board of Arbitration as hereinafter described, within thirty calendar days.

cont'd

18.10 The Union may file a grievance alleging violation, mis-interpretation or non-application of any provision of this Agreement. Such a grievance will be entered by the President or Secretary of the Union Local, with the Manager of Union Relations who, within 48 hours, will notify the Union at which stage the grievance will be processed.

ARTICLE 19
Arbitration

19.01 Failing settlement under the grievance procedure set forth in Article 18 hereof of any grievance between the parties or any employee's grievance, arising from the interpretation, application, non-application or violation of any of the provisions of this Agreement, including any question as to whether a matter is arbitrable, such may be referred to arbitration within thirty (30) days. Within seven (7) days of the notice of election to arbitrate each of the parties shall select a representative and the two so selected shall designate a third member of the board, who shall act as chairman. In the event that the two representatives originally selected shall be unable to agree on the third member within seven (7) working days of their appointment, the Minister of Labour for the Province of Ontario shall have the power, on the application of the parties hereto to appoint an impartial chairman.

19.02 The unanimous or majority decision of the Board of Arbitration with respect to matters coming within the jurisdiction of the Board pursuant to the provisions of this Agreement, shall be final and binding on both parties hereto, and should be rendered within seven (7) working days from the time the matter was referred to the Board.

19.03 Such Board of Arbitration shall have no jurisdiction to alter, change, amend or enlarge, the terms of this Agreement.

19.04 Expenses which may be incurred in connection with the Chairman will be borne equally by both parties to this Agreement.

19.05 Where applicable, a grievance, when posted for arbitration, shall state the Article and Sections of this Agreement which it has alleged have been breached.

cont'd

ARTICLE 22
Check-Off

22.01 During the term of this Agreement the Company will continue to recognize dues deduction authorization cards of present employees and will deduct in accordance therewith for each pay period of two weeks an amount equivalent to Union Dues, except as otherwise provided in this Article.

22.02 An employee hired or entering the bargaining unit during the term of this Agreement will be required within 30 days after his date of employment or transfer to complete an Employee's Check-Off Card (in the form set out in Appendix "B") assigning to the Union, through payroll deductions, an amount equivalent to that provided under 22.01. The same requirements shall apply to any present employee within 30 days after date of this Agreement for whom no Employee Check-Off Card is on record with the Company.
An employee who has revoked such authorization pursuant to Clause 22.03 shall, on the effective date of this Agreement have such authorization reinstated.

22.03 When the dues deduction authorization card has been signed by the employee and deposited with the Company, in accordance with 22.05, deduction will be made, in accordance with the provisions of this Article, for the term of this Agreement and any extension or renewal thereof, subject, however, to the employee having the absolute right to revoke such authorization at any time within the 10-day period immediately preceding the expiration of this Agreement or renewal thereof. During this time an employee may leave with the Employment Office a notice thereof, in the form as set out in Appendix "C", which will become effective immediately. Upon receipt of such notice, the Company will notify the Union of the employees who have so revoked such dues deduction.

22.04 Upon written authorization from an employee (in the form set out in Appendix "B") the Company will deduct an initiation fee of $5.00.

22.05 Dues deduction authorization cards must be presented either by an employee signing the card or by the chief steward, or by a departmental steward deputized by

cont'd

the chief steward, to the Employment Office, at which time the employee's signature will be verified and his identity established satisfactorily to the Company.

22.06 There will be no coercion or intimidation of any employee by either the Company or the Union in regard to the dues deduction arrangement.

22.07 Union dues are deductible in each pay period for which an employee receives pay, except where such pay is insufficient to cover dues deduction in which cases the omitted deduction will be recovered in the next pay period in which there is sufficient pay.

22.08 The Union agrees to keep the Company harmless from any claims against it by an employee which arise out of deduction under this Article.

22.09 An employee who returns to work from lay-off, sickness or leave of absence of who re-enters the bargaining unit, shall have current deductions automatically reinstated upon return to work, except as otherwise provided in this Article.

22.10 It is agreed that before an employee enters the bargaining unit the chief steward, or a departmental steward deputized by the chief steward, shall have the right to interview such employee during a five-minute period, at a time and place to be designated by the Company. The expense of such interview will be borne by the Union.

ARTICLE 23
Representatives

23.01 The Union shall supply the Company with the names of those employees who have been elected Union Officers, Grievance Committee men, Stewards, and Union Job Evaluation Panel members, authorized to represent the Union, and the Union shall keep such lists up-to-date and the Company advised accordingly.

23.02 The Company will supply the Union with the names, titles and departments of foremen, superintendents and representatives of the Personnel Department Staff who may be called upon to act with respect to the administration of this Agreement. Such information will be supplied to the Union on the occasion of the signing of the Agreement and on a quarterly basis thereafter.

cont'd

ARTICLE 24
Information to the Union

24.01 Copies of all notices which are posted on the plant bulletin boards, which deal with hours, wages or working conditions, will be sent to the President of the Local Union.

ARTICLE 25
Notices

25.01 The Company agrees to post in its plant, Union notices announcing Union meetings or social events, subject to the following conditions:
   a. Such notices shall first receive the stamped approval of the Company prior to posting.
   b. No change shall be made in any such notice, either by the Company or by the Union, after it has received the stamped approval of the Company.

25.02 The Union will not distribute or post or cause or permit to be distributed or posted on the property of the Company, for or on its behalf, any pamphlets, advertising or political matter, cards, notices, or other kinds of literature except with the written permission of the Company.

ARTICLE 26
Jury Duty

26.01 An employee who is called for Jury Duty will receive for each day of absence therefor the difference, between pay lost, computed at the employee's hourly wage rate and the amount of jury fee received, provided that the employee furnishes the Company with a certificate of service signed by the Clerk of the Court, showing the amount of jury fee received.

ARTICLE 27
Bereavement Pay

27.01 Subject to the following regulations the Company will make payment of wages to an employee who is absent solely due to a death in his immediate family.
   a. Such employee must have completed sixty (60) worked days.
   b. Such employee except for the death and funeral would otherwise be at work.

cont'd

27.02 Members of the employee's immediate family are defined for the purposes of this Agreement as spouse, son, daughter, father, mother, sister, brother, father-in-law and mother-in-law.

27.03 An employee will receive payment for the time lost from his regularly scheduled hours on the following basis:
a. Payment will be made on the basis of the employee's hourly wage rate for the employee's regularly scheduled shift up to 8 hours per day, exclusive of overtime and other forms of premium pay, for up to three day's absence.
b. The time to be paid for may be any three consecutive working days from the day of death through the day after the funeral, inclusive.
c. When requested by the Company, the employee will furnish satisfactory proof of death of the member of his immediate family.

27.04 An employee will not be eligible to receive payments under this Agreement for any period in which he is receiving other payments in the form of vacation pay, specified holiday pay, disability benefit, or Workmen's Compensation.

ARTICLE 28
Duration and Termination

28.01 This Agreement shall remain in effect until Dec. 31, 1978, and unless either party gives to the other party written notice of termination or of its desire to amend the Agreement, then it shall continue in effect for a further year without change.

28.02 Notices that amendments are required or that either party intends to terminate the Agreement may only be given within a period of ninety to seventy days prior to the expiration of this Agreement.

28.03 If notice of amendment or termination is given by either party, the other party agrees to meet for the purpose of negotiating such proposals within fifteen days after the giving of such notice, if requested so to do. Such negotiations shall not continue beyond the expiration date of the Agreement or extension unless the parties mutually agree to extend the period of negotiations.

cont'd

APPENDIX "A"
Labour Grade Job Rates and
Progression Step Rates
Effective: Jan. 1, 19–

Schedule #1

Labour Grade	Job Rate	Start Rate	After 3 Months	After 6 Months
1-1	$5.369	$5.369	$ —	$ —
1-2	5.472	5.369	5.472	—
1-3	5.577	5.472	5.577	—
1-4	5.681	5.577	5.681	—
1-5	5.797	5.681	5.797	—
1-6	5.924	5.797	5.924	—
1-7	6.039	5.797	5.924	6.039
1-8	6.187	5.924	6.039	6.187
1-9	6.390	6.039	6.187	6.390
1-10	6.576	6.187	6.390	6.576
1-11	6.751	6.390	6.576	6.751
1-12	6.942	6.576	6.751	6.942
1-13	7.193	6.751	6.942	7.193
1-14	7.407	6.942	7.193	7.407

Schedule #2

Labour Grade	Job Rate	Start Rate	After 3 Months	After 6 Months
2-1	$5.265	$5.265	$ —	$ —
2-2	5.340	5.265	5.340	—
2-3	5.425	5.340	5.425	—
2-4	5.505	5.425	5.505	—
2-5	5.579	5.425	5.505	5.579
2-6	5.674	5.505	5.579	5.674
2-7	5.759	5.579	5.674	5.759

NOTE: The final digit of the Job Code of a job classification indicates the applicable wage schedule.

cont'd

APPENDIX "B"
Employee's Check-Off Card

I authorize the Company to deduct from each pay period of two weeks an amount equivalent to Union dues and to remit the same promptly to the Financial Secretary of the union.

I understand that this authorization is binding on me commencing from the date hereof subject to my right to revoke such authorization within a 10-day period immediately preceding the expiration date of the Agreement or renewal thereof.

Date _____

Signature _____

Department _____

Badge No. _____

I also authorize the Company to deduct from my next first pay of the month, the sum of $5.00 for my Union initiation fee.

Date _____

Signature _____

APPENDIX "C"
Dues Deduction Cancellation

I hereby authorize and direct the Company to discontinue immediately the deduction from each pay period of two weeks an amount equivalent to Union dues, authorized by me pursuant to the Agreement between the Company and the Union.

Signature _____

Address _____

Badge No. _____

INDEX

Promotion, 9

Records, personnel, 90:
    retention of, 91, 92, 93, 107
Recruiting, 9 (see also
    Selection decision and
    Applicants)
Recruiting strategy, 28:
    and tactics, 168
Reference Checking Form, 73
References, 72
Replacement cost, 19:
    worksheet, 19
Resumes, 42
Return on Investment, 17
Rewards, non-financial, 137
Rules for discipline, 151, 152;
    Pot-bellied stove, 151, 152

Schools, colleges, universities, 35
Screening, 59
Selection by motivation, 31
Selection decision, 75
Seniority (union contract), 200
Sources of applicants, 34
Standards:
    of employment (legal), 94
    engineered, 8
    non-engineered, 8
    performance of, 4, 5, 9
Standards worksheet, 9, 10
Stewards, union, 208
Supervising handicapped
    persons, 85
Supervisor's role in job
    enrichment, 146
Suspension grievances
    (union contract), 207

Technological change (union
    contract), 199
Termination (dehiring), 106, 180
Tests, 74
Theft, 159
Training and development, 110:
    apprenticeship, 113
    Canada Employment
        Commission, 113
    methods of, 112
    on-the-job, 112
    responsibility for, 111
Transfer, 9

Turnover, 160:
    desirable, 170
    policy and strategy for, 166
    and recruiting strategy
        and tactics, 168
    (short term), 169
    (long term), 170
Turnover Costs Worksheet, 167
Turnover Planning Worksheet, 165
Turnover Worksheet, 160, 161, 162

Unions, 38:
    collective bargaining, 181
    example of collective
        agreement, 185, 189
    arbitration, 212
    bereavement pay, 215
    check-off, 213, 218
    discharge and suspension
        grievances, 207
    duration and termination, 216
    grievances, 209
    holidays, 195
    hours of work and overtime,
        193
    jury duty, 215
    leave of absence, 206
    management rights, 191
    probationary employees, 205
    representatives, 214
    seniority, 200
    shift bonus, 199
    stewards, 208
    technological change, 199
    vacation pay, 195
    wages, 197, 217
    how they work, 185
    Labour Relations Act, 183
    why employees join, 182

Vacation pay, 101:
    in union contract, 195

Wage, minimum, 96
Wages and salaries, 125:
    procedure for setting, 128
    in union contract, 197, 217
Workmen's Compensation Act
    (personnel records), 93

Young employees, 78